ANOTHE

By the Author of

A KIND OF MAGIC

ANOTHER KIND OF MAGIC

Mollie Harris

Illustrated by
JOHN WARD, R.A.
and
JOHN SERGEANT

Oxford   New York
OXFORD UNIVERSITY PRESS
1985

Oxford University Press, Walton Street, Oxford OX2 6DP

London New York Toronto
Delhi Bombay Calcutta Madras Karachi
Kuala Lumpur Singapore Hong Kong Tokyo
Nairobi Dar es Salaam Cape Town
Melbourne Auckland

and associated companies in
Beirut Berlin Ibadan Mexico City Nicosia

Oxford is a trade mark of Oxford University Press

First published 1971 by Chatto and Windus
First issued as an Oxford University Press paperback 1985

British Library Cataloguing in Publication Data
Harris, Mollie
Another kind of magic.
1. Cotswold Hills (England)——Social life and customs
I. Title
942.4'170858   DA670.C83
ISBN 0-19-281858-9

Library of Congress Cataloging in Publication Data
Harris, Mollie.
Another kind of magic.
(Oxford University Press paperback)
1. Cotswold Hills (England)——Anecdotes, facetiae,
satire, etc.   2. Harris, Mollie.   I. Title.
DA670.C83H37 1985   942.4'17   84-29495
ISBN 0-19-281858-9 (pbk.)

Printed in Great Britain by
Richard Clay (The Chaucer Press) Ltd
Bungay, Suffolk

To Mont
with grateful thanks

Some parts of this book were originally published in *The Witney Gazette*. 'Ship Dags' appeared in *The Countryman*, and many of the characters' anecdotes have been broadcast on the B.B.C. in country magazine programmes.

CONTENTS

DIALECT WORDS AND DEFINITIONS

narn—none

summut—something

twunt—it won't be

wunt—won't know, will not know

uffor—before

gaiger—pint

mumchancing—dreaming, thinking

forrod—forward

ju—do you

cackle—chatter

tud—it would

clapered—stuck up with muck or mud

grammard—grimed

lappen—fool

youn—yours

wass—what's

traipsin—walking

yead—head

sin—seen

nuss—nurse

erd—she'd

pressure—impression

dang—darn or damn

thur—there

ud—would

pritnear—pretty near

wur—where

allus—always

fust—first

gyardener—gardener

yer—here

smamsed—smothered, mucked up

knawed—knew or known

fuddled—bewildered, muddled

cyart—cart

ower—our

owern—ours

fer—for

tith—teeth

farty—forty

awf—off

yen it—isn't it

flommoxed—worried or bothered

ent—have not

ship dags—sheep dags—wool and manure

kidly byen—kidney beans

claggum—mucky or sticky

bwoy—boy

ketch—catch

arter—after

ent—are not

gyet—gate

gyets—get

yent—isn't

byent—are not

bisent—am not

twunt—it won't

stwon—stone

burrowness—shelter, in the burrow

issday—yesterday

ship—sheep

shupperin—shepherding

missling—fine rain

Introduction

Another Kind of Magic is about Cotswold Country and some of the people who live there. I was born and brought up on its nearby ridges and love every fold and hill, from wherever the experts say it begins and ends. For my part it seems to start rising very gradually just a few miles from my home.

But the first real breath of Cotswold air, clear and sharp as wine, meets me when I journey through Woodstock; then, about half a mile from the houses, going north in the direction of Chipping Norton, suddenly I seem to be in a different world and to use old Mark's expression ' 'Tis a jackut colder this side of Woodstock'. From then on in winter the visitor needs to button his jacket to the top, for now he has entered much colder, exhilarating country where, according to the old rhyme 'the wind blows so cold that the cooks can't cook their dinner'.

INTRODUCTION

But however chilly it may seem it is surely some of the loveliest country in England. In any season Cotswold country is delightful, whether shrouded in mist and rain, snow and ice, clad in the cool green of early summer or the brilliant patchwork of autumn when field and hedgerow, stubble and furrow, each throw up a different hue. Then there's the dry walling that runs for miles and miles, which is the method used for parting the fields, a method which has lasted for hundreds of years, outliving fences and hedges, besides providing shelter from the cold winds for stock and young lambs; humans too can find 'burrowness' behind these walls especially at 'victual' time.

In *Another Kind of Magic* you too can meet some of the delightful Cotswold characters that I have met. It has been a great privilege to have known them—their country wit may not be as quick as the townsman's, but it is there—they have a knack of bringing it out, more slowly perhaps, but with more meaning than their subtle town cousins. You may feel that you would like to meet some of the people that I have written about—my advice to you is, *save your energy*.

There are still people living in the Cotswolds who would fit the description of my characters, and rather than expose my friends I have disguised them. But this book is a tribute to them: those wise, wonderful people of the hills, who can teach us much.

A COTSWOLD SHEPHERD

IT was a fine Autumn morning—heavy with mist, an almost certain promise that the day later on would be hot and sunny. I cycled off to see my old shepherd friend Mark—a letter from him had read: 'Look out for a big flock of sheep, your side of Chippy—you can't miss us, we be nine hundred odd.' Actually there's a thousand sheep in the flock, but like most shepherds he considers it unlucky to give an actual figure.

The swirling mist seemed to get thicker as I travelled higher, then quite suddenly only the valleys were shrouded, the rolling hilltops quite clear. A few fields away I could see the flock. I peddled off down into the valley again for a little way. Soon I felt the gradual climb but couldn't see much yet, but quite plainly could hear the sheep and one of the dogs—the old one I think it was. I got off my bike and walked, climbing higher. Suddenly, bursting out of the mist, there they were—nine hundred odd sheep and Mark looking like the Good Shepherd himself right in the middle of them. He wasn't carrying a lamb, but tending to an animal who seemed to have yards and yards of blackberry bramble twined round and round its body.

The wide grin, the twinkling blue eyes, the face ruddy with over sixty years of Cotswold air, greeted me.

'Dang me if I could see you a-comin', but I knawed as somebody was about, my old dog kept tryin' to tell I.'

The dog nuzzled up to him as if to say: 'See, I told you somebody was coming.'

Mark took out his huge pocket watch. Automatically he rubbed its face with his thumb.

'You be just come right—'tis victual time.'

We made a bee line for the hut, the dogs following close at Shup's heels.

'They knaws 'tis victual time too,' he said, jerking his head in the dogs' direction. 'We 'en't 'ad narn a bite since six.'

The hut was clean and tidy and smelled of sweet summer hay, clover scented and warm. In one corner there were the medical supplies for the sheep— several tins of one thing and another for the prevention of many of the diseases that can attack the flock. On a large nail was a bundle of cut string, the coarse bag-tie sort for tying up wire and hurdles. Several old coats were draped over the hay-bales to dry— there were wellingtons, waterproof leggings, a spare cap and a huge wooden block—it looked like a chopping block. This was Shup's seat. I noticed that he had neatly folded a couple of sacks and placed them on the top.

Catching my glance he said, 'Tha's in your honour—my backside's used to settin' on hard places.'

I took a seat while Mark sat down on a huge tin of sheep dip; the dogs waited outside the open door. He threw them a handful of biscuits.

It gives Shup the greatest pleasure to supply me with food when I visit him. He would have felt very hurt had I brought my own or refused his. Out of his bag he fetched the top of a cottage loaf, new and crusty. It was already cut through the middle. Another piece of paper revealed two lumps of cold bacon. Shup shared this between us. 'Yer be,' he said, 'that'll stick to yer ribs—wants a good bit of fat on yer entrails in this climate.'

Out came Mark's pocket knife. Holding his food in the left hand, he carefully cut a small wedge of bread and placed it under his left thumb—this was to keep the meat in place and to keep the food clean.

'Tha's what we calls a "thumb bit" in these parts,'

he told me, the first time I saw him do it. Then with his sharp penknife he skilfully slivered off bread and meat in one swipe, putting it into his mouth with the right hand which still held the knife. I had visions of him poking his eye out with his knife blade, but realised he had been doing this too long to have an accident.

For a few minutes we munched away in silence. Then old Mark said, 'Tha's a thing as dun't taste like it used to, my wench—bacon. Never do this shop tackle taste like that as we used to cure ourselves. Why, when we was all young boy-chaps livin' at home my old dad allus kept a couple of pigs. We was brought up on taters and bacon. Thur was nine 'a we boys—all gret strappin' chaps we was too— ah—taters and bacon was our mainstay, and our mother cooked a bucket of spuds every day and thur was plenty of greens and swedes to fill us up. I don't think we ever went short of a bit of grub.

'You see, my wench,' Mark went on, throwing the thumb bit to the dogs, 'my father was head gardener up at the big house—my word he did grow some crops too—both for the squire and for we at home.'

I smiled and leant my back against the side of the hut. The sun's warmth had penetrated the wood. It was peaceful and quiet high up on these wide rolling hills. I could listen to Mark for hours. He had not lost his wonderful dialect and spoke a different tongue to most of the people in that lovely valley where the river Glyme wends its way toward the great lake at Blenheim.

Mark rambled on, 'It was like this you see, my wench, my father and the squire got on terrible well together, thought the world of him 'e did, treated him more like a friend than a worker.

'But at this particular time as I be tellin' you about, the squire was fair flummoxed—somebody was takin' his prize peaches, as fast as they ripened they disappeared.

'He'd already asked the local bobby, P.C. Jones, to 'ave a look in during the hours of darkness, but they couldn't seem to catch the culprit red-handed.

'So my father volunteered to sit up one night and keep watch—squire thought this was a very good idea, they never told a soul of what they planned to do in case it warned the thief away. That night the squire kept watch till half-past eleven, then my old dad took over.

' "You go off to bed, sir," he said, "I shall be all right sittin' in this yer greenhouse."

'But the time did drag so—sittin' still's hard work to an active man. Then about four o'clock in the mornin' my old dad sees somebody sculkin' around, twas still pretty dark and he soon lost sight of who-ever it was.

'Out of his hidin' place comes me dad and up he went to the nearest peach tree, he picked a couple of

'um and was just stuffin' 'um into his pocket when a
heavy hand dropped on his shoulder and the gruff
voice of P.C. Jones said, "Ahh catched you this time,
my man, ho ho, look who we've got here, this is the
trusted head gardener who wouldn't pinch a pin is
it, well, well, what's the squire going to say about
this then?"

'P.C. Jones marched my old dad up to the front
door of the big house and rang the bell, after a few
minutes a sleepy housekeeper let them in.

' "Fetch the squire at once, Ma'am," he ordered,
"we've got the culprit at last. Look what I found on
him," he said, holding the two peaches in his hand.

'Course the squire couldn't believe his eyes when
he saw me old dad held by the red-faced policeman.

' "Do you wish to make a charge, sir?" asked
P.C. Jones. "Caught him red-handed I did."

'He didn't answer him but turned to my father
and said, "You can go home now, Jacob, but I shall
expect an explanation in the morning."

' "No time like the present, sir," broke in my
dad quickly. Then he took a mighty sweep at P.C.
Jones's helmet—it crashed to the floor and out of it
rolled half a dozen of the squire's best peaches.

'Mind you, the squire didn't prosecute, but that
finished P.C. Jones. He was sacked from the force
and never spoke to my father again he didn't.'

I glanced at Mark. He was back in his youth

again. His blue eyes had a far-away look—he was back in his hard, happy childhood of long ago. He caught my glance.

'Yer be I mumchancin' and no Friday pen up yet.'

Out came the huge watch, 'Time we was out in the field again. I likes to get a bit forrod with me pennin'—then by Friday afternoon I got me Sat'day and Sunday pen up. We can go on chattrin' while I works.'

Out with the flock again—we blinked in the brilliant sunshine. The sheep were grazing on cocksfoot grass. It had been cut in the early summer, but the wet season had produced a good crop, long and lush, so that the sheep had to be penned off on so much of it a day.

The speed at which Mark worked was amazing, and rolls of wire and hurdles were quickly fixed to the stakes which he whacked in the ground with his great crowbar (folding bar), while nimble fingers tied string to the posts.

The huge flock were a cross between Cheviot sheep and Border Leicesters, a much smaller variety than Mark had been used to shepherding.

'Are you getting more used to looking after this type of sheep,' I asked him, knowing full well that his heart was still with the old breed of Cotswold's.

''Tis a matter of havin' to get used to 'um, the ladies don't want a lot of fat meat these days, spoils thur figgers they all ses, but fer meself I allus did fancy both ship an' women with a good bit a fat on 'um.

'Do you knaw when you slapped a Cotswold ship on the rump, that was just like hittin' a quarten of dough, they was so fat.

'Still, even a shupperd has to move with the times, bless me soul, 'twassen't no good I a-sayin' as I couldn't look arter nothin' but Cotswolds, fer they be gone right out of fashion.

'They do say as there's only one flock left in the country, and they be kept on a farm 'tother side of Burford. 'Ent you ever sin 'um? Like young donkeys they looks when they be a-grazin'.

'Of course, 'twas quantity not quality that was produced years ago. Nowadays folks be more finicky about thur clothes—what man or woman wants to wear anything made out of that coarse wool what comes from they Cotswold ship, that all goes to the making of carpets and rugs. 'Tis wool from this sort of ship,' he went on, burying his great knarled hand in the lovely thick sheep's back, 'that you ladies likes for knittin'.

'But the fleeces from these yer cross-breds be only half the weight as they we used to have off the Cotswold ship. I've knawed the time when it only took two of 'um to weigh a Tod—thas roughly twenty-eight pounds.'

As Shup dismantled the pen that the sheep had

finished with, I noticed, when he pulled a stake from the ground, that he quickly heeled in the hole.

'What do you do that for?' I asked him. I was fast learning more about sheep than ever before, but I didn't know why he did this.

'Well now, if I left holes like that all over the field I might have half the flock wi' broken legs, 'cos they'll graze this grass again when we've bin over it once. You see if I didn't heel the holes in they ship be just as likely to get thur foot stuck down 'um, and the dogs might do the same thing. And no shuppurd can risk that—nothin' upsets a man more than to have summut 'appen to his flock that could have bin avoided.

'But goin' back to Cotswold ship,' he went on, 'my old grandfather used to tell I that when they 'ad the ship fairs at Stow, thur 'ud be as many as twenty thousand ship thur and most of 'um Cotswolds, the rest was Welsh. A wonderful sight 'e said it was too—you see thur's five main roads that meets at Stow-on-theWold—just picture it, thousands of ship pourin' into that town from all the countryside around—ah, must 'ave bin a wonderful sight an' no mistake.'

'Is that the reason you became a shepherd and not a gardener like your father?' I asked him.

'Ah, I suppose 'twas because I spent a lot of time wi' me grandparents, I was the oldest you see, and me parents was glad fer I to go and stop with 'um sometimes—left a bit more room for they as was left at home. They do say as I be the spittin' image of me grandfather—my word he was a wonderful story-teller, he'd sit fer hours and tell I such wonderous things, I'll tell 'e about 'um sometime, when we got a bit more time.'

Not that Mark was still for a moment while he'd been chattering. His enormous hands were tying string to hurdles as neatly and quickly as a boy scout. He was a huge man—well over six feet tall—and he walked with a long springy stride, so that I had some difficulty in keeping up with him. He must cover miles a day—dismantling pens and putting up new ones, always keeping two days in advance with the pens. All day long he was bending—whacking—rolling up, tying up, and rolling out again, great bundles of fencing wire, as well as keeping a look out for any sick animals in the great flock. We gazed at the sheep—but to me every one looked the same; a sort of vacant look they all had which reminded me of a long-nosed white-faced maiden aunt of ours.

'No, they be all different,' Mark said when I remarked on the similarity. 'If any of these was put wi' another flock I could pick mine out in a minute, I knaws everyone of 'um.'

The Friday pen was now completed, and we stood on top of the hill drinking in the glorious scenery. The day was clear, warm and sparkling, the elms already tinged with Autumn gold.

'See that big clump of trees over there,' Mark said, pointing his long arm westerly, 'see, right on the skyline.' I followed the finger and found the clump.

'Yes—yes—I've got it, is it a special wood?' I asked.

'No—tha's just a covert of beech trees—beech grows well on these hills, but that big clump happens to be over thirty mile away on the old Stow-London road, the old drovers road we calls it.'

The arm swung round easterly. 'Ju knaw what that hill is then?' Two pairs of narrowed eyes were focused on the clear horizon miles and miles away. 'Tha's Cumnor Hill, Oxford, that is—mind you, that has to be clear affor that shows up like it do today.

'And behind these yer trees,' he went on, inclining his head, 'is the circus.'

I grinned. 'Go on, you're pulling my leg.'

'Tha's gospel,' he said; 'tha's what they calls thur winter quarters, but thurs somebody thur all the year round. They do say as thurs lions an' all sorts foreign animals penned up thur. Mind you, I takes perticler notice as I don't go by thur; I don't want to get 'et to death. I hopes to live long and die 'appy, and not end up wi' bein' fodder fer a lot of wild animals,' he chuckled.

'And back behind us, thurs nothin'—thurs nothin'ness between yer and Banbury.'

ANOTHER KIND OF MAGIC

I turned and gazed at the expanse of rolling hills.
What Mark meant was, there was no landmark—
nothing but miles and miles of green, gold and
brown—lush, unspoilt Cotswold country, beautiful,
and bountiful.

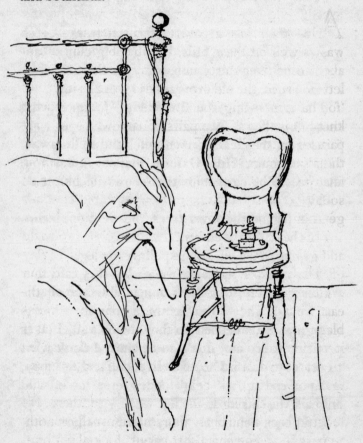

2

'ME OPERATION'

AS a rule Mark only writes to me when he and the flock have moved a fair distance away, so I was surprised to see that I'd got a letter from him about a month after my last visit. It was rather a sad letter. He hadn't moved far but wrote to say that 'for the past week I've bin feeling so bad, I don't know how I gets through the day—I be in such pain—reckons I'll have to go and see the old quack, the rains getting I down too. I've had a wet shirt a few times lately, I've had nine top coats and macs all sobbled'd up and not one of them fit to put on, can't get them dry quick enough.'

I knew that he must be feeling pretty bad to write and tell me, for in all his year's he'd never had a day off for illness, so although the day was cold and missling with rain I set off to see him. The south-east wind cut across the Cotswold hills like a knife-blade, and the rain was so sharp and cold it felt as if it was making holes in my face; but the air was invigorating and I felt quite fresh and elated as I rode along.

Mark was sitting in the hut when I got there. He looked pinched and blue; his eyes that usually sparkle were dull, and he had a sort of hurt look about him.

In the hut, jackets and coats hung wet, dismal and dripping. The dogs came out from under the hut looking absolutely fed up with the bad weather and their unusually quiet master.

'You shouldn't a' come out yer on a day like this my wench, look at yu', you be all sobbled'd up wi' wet.'

'Never mind about me—a drop of rain won't hurt. Now what's this all about you feeling groggy,' I asked.

I could tell Mark was in pain. During these few minutes his hand had gone to his side more than once and he winced as he talked.

'Reckons it 'ave beat I this time gel. As soon as I've had a wash an' shave I shall go along to see the old quack tonight.'

I noticed that Mark didn't even want to smoke, so I knew he must be feeling pretty bad. He promised he'd let me know in the next few days how things were with him.

Four days after my trip to see Mark I got a letter from him, but it was postmarked Oxford. I ripped it open and was surprised to see not his usual home address but 'Radcliffe Infirmary' in spidery scrawl. The letter read:

This is a bit of a shock for you my wench. 'Twas for I too, but I've had it now and its all over. When I got home that night after you'd been to see I, I'm damned

if I could move, so our Fred goes off for the Doctor and
he soon had I in that ambulance and I was in Oxford
before you could say 'Jack Robinson'. . . . Could you
come in and see I and I'll tell you all the news.

From where I stood in the corridor I could see
Mark propped up in bed. A little nurse came out and
opened the doors and said 'Visiting time' and we all
trouped in to part off at the various beds in the ward.
Mark caught sight of me and blushed like a youngster as I went up to him.

He was certainly in better shape than when I'd
seen him last and chattered incessantly for the
whole half-hour that I was there.

The man in the next bed didn't have anyone to see
him and I was being sort of shared between them
both. 'This is 'er as I tell'd 'e about Joe,' Mark said
to his neighbour. Joe grinned—a quiet little man
Joe seemed, anyhow he let Mark do most of the
chattering. Only when visiting time was up did Joe
have anything to say.

'A master fellow he is' he went on jerking his
head in Mark's direction. 'I've never laughed so
much in all my life as I have since he came round
after his operation. Doctors and nurses all seem to
like him and he says unbelievable things to them—
he's making us all laugh all day. If he goes home
before I do I shan't half miss him.'

I bade my two invalids goodbye with a promise

to come again soon. Before I was out of the ward Mark was making the night nurse laugh. The sister remarked to me, 'He's a merry fellow that one—how pleasant life would be if all our patients were so happy' and she bustled off—stiff backed—rustling with starch.

One or two things cropped up within the next few days and before I had time to go to Oxford again there was another letter from Mark to say that 'I be off home on Wednesday, so if you don't come to see I before then I shall be at home'.

I waited a few days before setting out to see Shup again. Country folk love visitors of all kinds but there is a sort of reserve about them, I knew; for a little while Mark would like to get settled. I would let the family and near neighbours be the first to hear all the 'horrible details' of the trip to Oxford. Only when the excitement had died down a little would it be my place to visit him. So after he'd been home about a week I made my way over the hills once more and knocked at the door of his cottage. Getting no reply I went along to Shup's neighbour whose name I've never heard for he always refers to her as 'Missus next door'.

'I've come to see how Mark is' I explained to her after we'd said our good mornings. 'I've knocked at the door but couldn't make him hear. Perhaps he's still in bed?'

'In bed Missus, no that 'e en't—thur was no

'oldin' 'im once 'e got 'ome. Farmer 'ad to take 'im
up to see the sheep as soon as 'e come out a 'ospital
and 'e bin a goin' up thur every day since—not for
all day, mind you, for 'e en't well yet, not be a long
chalk 'e en't.'

She gave me the direction to the field where Old
Shup would be—he certainly was a marvel to be out
'shupperin' as he called it, so soon after his operation.

As always, he was pleased to see me. I try to
arrange to visit him during his dinner time, otherwise his boss might think I was encouraging Shup
to waste time. Not that the old fellow would do
that, for he belongs to the old school and has his
own ideas about employees who don't give value
for money.

Our dinner consisted of bread and cheese. I declined a huge raw onion that Mark offered, but the
hot sweet cocoa that we swilled it down with was
very welcome.

The conversation came round to operations and
it wasn't long before I was rolling with laughter at
some of the antics that he'd got up to in hospital.

'I reckons as 'ow they nusses used to get I goin'
a purpose just to 'ear I a chatterin'. Course 'alf the
time they couldn't understand me cackle, strikes me
they en't never 'ad anybody from this part a the
country affor—leastways tha's what I thinks.

'I wasn't feeling too bad when I fust got thur and

I an' a few more had to wait in a little room fer a while, till they got the beds made I suppose.

'Well we be set thur a chatterin'—every one of us was worse that t'other be all accounts. Then a little nuss says "I shan't call Mr. Adams again, I know he's one of you—now you just answer up". Then I thought to meself, tha's I—I en't never bin called Mr. Adams fer this farty years—they all calls I "Old Shup" er "Old Mark". Then awf I goes tu see the one as they calls "sister". "Mr. Adams," 'er says, so I stops 'er an' I ses, "Look 'ere Ma'am I en't bin called that fer this farty odd years, cyan't you call I old Shup er Old Mark like everybody else do?"

'You should a sin 'er face. I thinks 'er'd a liked to 'ave laughed but I s'pose it en't proper to 'ob nob wi' patients.

'"Well now" she said, very sternlike "really I can't call you any of those names." Then she thought for a minute and said "I tell you what we'll call you—Mr. Mark—how will that do?" So I thanked 'er kindly and said 'tud do fine—so that was it. I was Mr. Mark tu all on 'em.

'Ahh an' byent they nusses some grand little gels too, smashin' little figgers they got—thur yent no wench in ower village that got a figger like what they got, dang me if thur is.

'Fust day I was thur, one on 'um comes an' puts a screen round I. "Whatever you done that for" I ses to 'er? "You're going to be examined by the doctor" she said. "Well" I ses to 'er "I dun't see as 'ow that screen's necessary at all. I byent no different to anybody else as I knows on", an' 'er went awf a chucklin' an' laughin' to 'erself.

'After a few minutes the old doctor bloke comes along, an' we 'as a long chat. Talk about questions! He asked I all sorts a things, so I ses to 'im arter we got a bit friendly like "Well sir, when be you goin' tu 'ave a go at I?", an' 'e said "Tomorrow I think will be best Mr. Mark". "Well then" I ses to 'im "Thee gyet that old knife sharpened up an' make a damned good clean cut on it—I dun't want none a this yer muckin' about." An' 'e laughed an' said "I'll do that—I'll see you tomorrow then Mr. Mark."

'So next morning they brings I one a they white coat things an' some long white socks. "Go along to the bathroom and put these on," some pretty little nuss said. Well that white coat thing only come up tu me knees an' thur wasn't no fastenin' on 'im so I puts 'im on, with the openin' down the front and goes walking down the ward. You should 'ave 'eard that sister, proper fiery 'er was. "Get back in that bathroom you disgusting man an put that blessed thing on properly with the split up the back." Well 'ow was I to know—I'd never bin to Oxford affor in me life, let alone 'ospital. 'Course the other chaps in the beds all busted out laughin',

proper uproar thur was fer a minute or two. Then I'd only got one a they white socks so out I goes agen "Sister" I ses "I thought I was goin' to 'ave me belly cut—not me foot" an' I 'olds me bare leg up to show 'er. That made 'er laugh. "Here's the other sock on your bed you silly man", her said to I.

'Well, awf I goes fer me operation an' affor I knows wur I be, I be back in bed wi' me belly that sore. One thing about 'ospitals they do let you 'ave a drop a beer. I 'ad 'alf a pint most nights, an' when I come round arter me operation that's the fust thing I asked for, and I got it.

'The old surgeon bloke comes to see I next day an' 'e ses "You're a remarkable man Mr. Mark. I hear that you insisted on getting out of bed and making a trip to the lavatory an hour after you came round from your operation!"

'"Well, sir," I said, "'tis like this. You see I byent used to women tha's the thing an' as fer settin' up in bed on one a they chamber things—well, I couldn't."

'Well, come the day when the farmer's wife—'e as I works fer—'er said 'er'd come and fetch I out at 11 o'clock. Then a message comes to say as 'er couldn't get thur till three. I was settin' out in me dressin' gown when the old doctor comes along.

' "Hello Mr. Mark," he said, "I thought you were gone home."

'So I ses to 'im, "I can't go wi'out me clobber can I?" "Without you what," he said.

' "Wi'out me clobber—me clothes" I told him, and he laughed and said, "I hope to see you again some time Mr. Mark."

'And I ses to 'im, "I 'opes to see you agen too sir, but I shan't come if you be goin' to chop I about agen." And 'e went down that corridor laughin' fit to bust 'isself.

'But I feels champion now, the Doctor said that

I should soon get well, because, 'e said I got a stummock as strong as a horse and I told 'im, no wonder, I 'as to work like one sometimes. Do you remember that awful winter we 'ad a few years back? That damned near killed I, and twas that what finished my old dog awf—he was goin' on fer fourteen you see and couldn't stand all the diggin' out we 'ad to do. That snowed fer days, the drifts was up to me shoulder—thas all we done my old dog and me was dig the ship out of snowdrifts— never lost one we didn't. I fell down twice, prit near done I was, but thur was nobody else to help, so I 'ad to pick meself up and get on with it. Tha's all we done they snowy days was feed the ship and dig 'um out of the drifts—ah some of 'um was eight and ten foot deep, I've never sin such snow all the time I bin shupperin'.

'But my wench, everything has its compensations —do you knaw the wool clip from ower ship the followin' summer was more than two tons—much more than we usually has. Nature has its own way of lookin' arter things and they ship growd more wool to help protect um.

''Course its allus a top coat colder up yer than 'tis 'tother side of Woodstock.'

3

AMOS AND ROSIE

CHRISTMAS had come and gone before I had a chance to visit Mark again. I'd had a long letter from him telling me where he had the sheep grazing, and a list of instructions on how to get to the outlandish place.

'When you get on the Chippy road, our side, look out for a signpost to Crowsford, turn right at Pee-wit corner and then left into White-way, turn right again at Will's grave, past a big field of brussel sprouts, a hundred yards past the sprouts there's a sharp turn left up a dark lane what we calls Hangman's Lane, we be up there.' These lovely country names were all right for the locals, but it was like double Dutch to me and I didn't see anyone to ask for miles and miles. It would be more by luck than judgement if I ever found Mark.

I was thinking of turning for home when I saw an old fellow out walking with his dog, but he was so deaf that I couldn't seem to make him understand what I wanted. I was just about to ride off again when he said 'You'd best come down and see the Missus, 'er 'ull tell you whatever it is you wants to know.'

Down the road and round a bend we went and, there in a clearing, stood a neat little cottage;

propped up against an old outhouse were bundles of faggots and some slim straight bean sticks, and stacked near the front door a pile of freshly sawn logs.

I left my bike outside the gate and we went up the small front garden path. The old fellow opened the door which led straight into a bright warm room. 'Rosie,' he called, 'Rosie come yer, there's a young 'oman as wants to know summut.'

The name certainly suited her—she was pink and rounded, she reminded me of the old-fashioned moss rose that grows in our garden. She had a pleasant serene look about her as she came from the back kitchen, wiping her soap-suddy hands on her apron.

'Hullc, Miss, can I do anything for you? It 'ent no good asking my Amos, fer 'es as deaf as a post, 'e don't understand a word you ses to him. Come on inside,' she went on, 'its enough to strip yu out there today, set down for a few minutes and I'll find summut to warm you both.'

She disappeared into the kitchen but was soon back with a bottle of home-made wine; she moved across to the dresser for glasses.

'This is a drop of me special,' she said pouring out the rich red wine, 'this will warm the cockles of your heart. This here is Sloe, I makes all sorts of the stuff, we drinks a lot of wine, tis like medicine you know as well as being warmful.'

Amos stood his on the hob. 'He likes to stand his there,' Rosie rambled on, friendly like, 'ses it takes the chill off. I has to watch as 'e don't put it too near, else he would crack the glass an' that's happened before now.'

We drank the clear heady wine. I declined a second offering. 'I'm not used to it at this time of the day,' I told her, 'it would go to the weakest place and that's my head,' and we laughed.

'I'll tell 'im what you said later on—he'll chuckle over that I'll be bound,' Rose said.

I explained where I was making for and asked her if she would put me on the right road.

'You'll be looking for Mark I'll bet, he that shepherds for Master Haines. Well now, you 'ent no more than two miles away from where he got the sheep—you was on the right road all right.'

I said goodbye to Amos—he and the dog were still thawing out by the wood fire. 'Who shall I tell Mark I've been visiting,' I asked Rose as we walked down the path to the gate.

'He'll know if you ses carter Townsend and his

missus, we've knowed Mark all his life, lived in the same village when we was younger and we've allus been friendly like.'

I set off again. The keen icy wind cut across from the east, but I was warmed with the good wine, a glowing fire and the welcome I had received from Amos and Rosie.

'I'll bet you had a job findin' we,' Mark said, 'I'd begun to give you up fer the day.'

I related my adventures to him. 'Ah-h course I knows 'um, I used to court Rosie at one time, and ower Fred used to be sweet on her sister what lives over at Campden. Funny thing,' he went on, 'none of we brothers married, though thurs plenty of time yet,' his eyes fairly danced, 'I might find one as suits I, if I looks hard enough,' he chuckled.

'I be just goin' to give the ship a bit extra grub— shouldn't be surprised if we don't get a fall of some sort, snow most likely, that winds got round east-ways this afternoon,' Mark said as we trudged over the sodden ground to the building where the sweet smelling hay was piled high.

'See, you never knows on these hills,' Mark went

on, cutting the string that held the tightly packed hay and releasing the smell of dried grass and summer flowers emblamed like tobacco flakes in the clumsy bales. 'You see my wench we mightn't be able to get yer for a day 'er so—not like the main roads; they clears quick with all the traffic on 'um. I've knowed the time when this very road 'ave bin blocked fer days. Course old Amos and his Missus be used to it, if you'd had a look in their larder you'd 'ave seen as they got thur supplies in ready, just in case we has some hard weather. They knows that they'll never get a baker's van er a milkman comin' along this yer narrow road just for a loaf of bread an' a pint of milk with the chance of gettin' stuck in a snowdrift, so they gets prepared like. And when we gets a lot of rain that cottage of their's floods summut dreadful—the water comes up through they stwon planks, sometimes they've come down in the mornin' and the chairs 'ave bin bobbin' about like corks. And did you notice they had got two or three of they home-made rag rugs on the floors, they sits a-makin' um most nights— well when that water rises a bit sudden like, they old rag rugs gets that sobbled up wi' water, old Rose got they hangin' out on 'e line fer weeks a-dryin'. But they don't want to move, 'ad the chance of a council house, but they won't go, they be got attached to that cottage they bin there that long. Course that's a tied cottage really, went with the cartering job, but old Amos's boss ses they can stop thur, you see none of the young farmworkers or thur wives want to live in an outlandish place like that with no conveniences er anything. So they lets um stay, the place would soon fall down if that was left empty fer long.'

Mark and I worked steadily along the field. I threw the hay bales from the back of the trailer while he drove at a snail's pace along the edge of the wire fence. We returned to the building for another load.

'I got a drop of tea left in me flask,' Mark said, diving into his dinner bag. And we sat down on the loaded trailer for a few minutes. Mark rolled himself a cigarette.

'I didn't tell you about the bad luck our gaffer had just affor Christmas did I? Well, you know 'e breeds a lot of turkeys—dang me if 'e didn't have about sixty of 'is stock birds pinched. Ah-h, three nights running somebody broke in. So old Fred Bailey, the farm foreman, suggested that two fellows ought to be on guard every night, well until after Christmas anyroad.

'And 'e said that 'e and 'is son would take the fust night's watch. And according to them this is what 'appened.

''Twas cold and frosty as Fred and his son Dick donned thur old army great-coats and Wellingtons; they pulled thur caps well down over thur ears, laced thurselves with half-a-pint of ten-year old dandelion wine and set off for the field, guns under thur arms.

'As they walked through the village they 'eard singing, coming from the pub it was too.

' "I'll bet tha's old Walt Tovey, I can recognise his melodious voice a mile off," Dick said. You see 'e was givin' 'um his special "Lille Marlene", and that being a clear frosty night made it sound louder. "We'd best get inside and 'ave half a pint 'er two affor we settles down hadn't us bwoy?" old Fred said, and thur was a roar of welcome as they went in; I knows cos I was set in thur with old Ned.

' 'Come on and have half a gaiger with I," he called to 'um, "theet want summut in yer insides to keep you warm if you be going to spend the night out in that field."

'Arter they'd had three or four pints, all the fore-man and his son did was brag about 'ow they was goin' to ketch the thieves red-handed. "We shall cop 'um tonight, you see if we don't, thur'll be no need for any of you others to keep watch, it'll all be over be mornin'," they said. "All we shall do is fire a few shots a bit low and scare the backside of 'um."

'They stuck in the pub till closing time, then made thur way off up to the field where the turkey arks was. It 'ad begun to snow—that nasty swirling blinding snow, the sort that gets you wet through in no time.

' "The best thing we can do" Fred said, "is to

park ourselves somewur so as we can see 'um come in the gyet (gate)—they got to come that way, thur yent no other way to get in the field. We cyant stop out in this weather bwoy", Fred went on, "we shall get buried in the snow at this rate, let's see if we can fix up some shelter of some sort." Then Dick had a brainwave.

' "If we was tu get in this yer ark, we should 'ave a clear view if anybody come in the field and we should be in the warm too."

'So they snuggled down along with 'alf-a-dozen fat cock birds; 'twas warm and close in thur and they was soon fast asleep.

'Suddenly Fred woke up—for a few moments he couldn't make out where he was—then 'e nudged his son—"Hey wake up bwoy," he said, "we be on the move."

'They, turkey arks and all, had been pinched and was halfway to London on the back of a lorry.

'It was a few minutes before they realised what was going on. Then Fred said, "What be us tu do now then bwoy? Shall us lay yer quiet till they stops somewur, then we can hold 'um at gunpoint, we still got the guns."

' "I got a better idea," Dick said, "If they two in the front was tu stop and go into a café, I could slip out and fetch a policeman smartish quick an' bring 'im back yer affor they makes awf agin."

'After a while the lorry drew up in a grimy back-

street, in a big town by the look of the buildings they thought. Both of the men in the front jumped down and went into a house.

' "Go on bwoy, make a run for it", Fred whispered, "And dun't ferget tu find out the name of the strit we be in, else you wunt know were tu come back tu."

46

'Dick crept out of the ark and up the dimly lit strit. Twas about three o'clock in the mornin' and not many folk about. After walking up a couple of strits he saw a phone box, dialled 999 and asked for the police. The night duty copper listened at the wild tale that the fellow on the phone was telling him. Course he thought twas somebody having a joke.

'Then Dick said a bit urgent like, "If you dunt send somebody quick tu Fernstack Road thur'll be murder dun when they turkey thieves come up 'gainst my old man, I tell 'e you'll 'ave tu 'urry up else somebody's going' tu get hurt."

' "You stay where you are young man," the policeman said, "and I'll send a patrol car round to pick you up and take you back to Fernstack Road, and don't do anything silly like shooting anybody."

'By the time the police got thur old Fred had got the thieves up agen the wall. He'd got 'is 12-bore gun held a bit close to 'um and was swearing summut terrible at the lorry driver and 'is mate.

'The police took charge of the thieves and asked Fred and Dick to go to the station too, and they'd see as they go back home all right.

'Then one of the turkey thieves turned to Fred and Dick and said, "how the devil you come to be so 'andy, to be here at the same time as we, did you follow us all the way up here?"

' "We followed you all right, only you brought us, we was in one a they turkey arks."

' "Well I'm b——" the other fellow said, "who'd a thought it, but now you comes to mention it, I thought that last b—— ark we put on the lorry was damned heavy."

'Ah, we've had many a laugh over that,' Mark said, shaking his head and chuckling.

All the time that he'd been telling me the turkey tale Mark had been busy feeding the sheep. The sky was already darkening and with a quick glance at the threatening clouds he said, 'See they little rough clouds there—they little uns, darker than the rest—they be messengers, and they be come to warn us that thur's bad weather a-comin', I'll bet we 'as snow by mornin.'

'Then I'd better get off home, tis nearly dark now,' I said, pulling on my gloves.

'Ah-h an' do that coat of yours up at the neck, you'll be froze to the marrow affor you gets far. Now you hurry awf 'ome, and you mark my words, tu'll be all white when you wakes up tomorrow.'

The weather certainly had changed since I'd started out, and my fingers were soon numb with cold.

When I woke the next morning the outside world was strangely quiet—no sharp sounds, just muffled noises of early morning in the village, and I knew before I opened my eyes that Mark had been right in his prediction—the countryside was covered in deep snow.

Rose's Sloe Wine

Pick 1 gallon of ripe sloes (usually late September or early October). Roll these in a damp cloth to clean them.

Place them in a pan and pour a gallon of boiling water over them. Now put in five pounds of *preserving* sugar, cover with a thick cloth and leave in the pan for fourteen days, stirring often. Strain and put the liquor in a cask or earthenware jar. Fermentation will now proceed slowly and while it continues corks or bungs should be kept fairly loose. When fermentation has ceased pour in a wine glass of brandy and ½ oz isinglass, then tighten up the bung or cork. Sloe wine takes a long time to mature so it is unwise to bottle it under a year. The longer you keep this wine the better it becomes.

4

SORTING SPUDS

THE February winds blew cold and damp as I made my way to Furlong barn, where some hundreds of tons of potatoes were stored, and where I was due to help with the potato sorting.

The sorting had probably been going on since the turn of the year at Glory Hill Farm, but now some of the men were needed to help get the land ready for planting, so the 'casuals' had been called in.

As I rode along I could see tractors bobbing across the fields. The ploughshares were cutting deep into the rich brown earth, lapping it over in thick dark layers, and there was that lovely unmistakable smell

of freshly turned soil. And following close behind the ploughs were hundreds of beautiful white gulls.

Some of the fields had been planted in the Autumn;

in these the winter wheat was already thrusting its way through the earth like millions of tiny green spears. The elm trees were already 'thickening' and would soon be showing their minute pink flowers. Catkins and Pussy Willow were blooming in the otherwise bare hedgerows and here and there in the grass the first few flowers of the Coltsfoot showed up bright and yellow.

As children we were afraid to pick these flowers. Our nickname for them was 'Pee the beds'. If this happened we should have got a walloping, so they were left to bloom and grow, untouched by most country children.

I look forward to a few weeks potato sorting. I know that I shall be working with my old friend Nellie Walker. Nellie is in her late fifties; she is short and fat and very jolly. She lives in one of the farm cottages along with her husband Harry and their twelve children.

They are a happy united family, and Nellie is a fine mother who loves each and every one of her offspring with a strong maternal pride. And Harry obviously adores his wife and brood with equal pride.

Up until a few years ago the farmer that we are working for, like others in this area, stored his potatoes in huge outside clamps. Nellie and I used to get 'frezzed stiff' as she called it. We had to stand out in the fields for six hours a day handling cold 'taters'. The east winds used to whip round us,

freezing us and numbing our hands and feet. When it snowed or rained, the work was at a standstill. But not any more. The walls in Furlong barn are a foot and a half thick. Its warm and dry in there and the work goes on all day and every day, uninterrupted by the weather.

Besides Nellie and myself there are three men in the sorting team. One man feeds the potatoes into the machine. He does this with a huge twelve tyned fork which is much wider than a garden fork. The prongs have small bulbous ends so that no damage is done to the crop, which quickly travels along two shaking trays. Here the potatoes lose any soil that might have been stuck on them, and at the same time the very small ones drop through to a separate container. The rest go up a fast moving elevator and it is here where our work starts. Nellie and I stand either side of the machine and we quickly snatch off any green or split potatoes which we drop into sacks that are hung by our sides. These potatoes are sold for pig-feed. Then the good clean ones travel on and drop into sacks which are fixed on to the end of the machine. The man working there has to move very quickly; he takes the full sacks off and clips empty ones back on. Another man is waiting to weigh off the hundredweight sacks and sew the tops up with the aid of a bagging needle and strong string. The third man stacks the full sacks in one ton lots.

We earn five shillings an hour—the same rate that we are paid for picking up the crop in the Autumn.

'Ah', Nellie told me one day, 'we was that hard up when we first got married that my Harry was glad to take any old job at the weekends. And one was to lift about three acres of taters fer another farmer. He had to dig 'um up with an ordinary garden fork *and* pick 'um up too. And what do you think he got paid fer doin' that?' she asked. 'A shillin' a sack full! Ah, 'e done that fer years, I used to help pick 'um up too. I'd take our Frankie and our Bobbie with me, that's me two eldest. They used to try and help, but they was more hindrance really, still the fresh air done 'um good.

'We was livin' about four miles from Painswick at the time, every such a lonely place it was, just one farmhouse and two cottages fer the workers. But they was good folk to work for; ah I reckon we stopped thur fer about ten years.

'One day I thought I'd give the kids a bit of a treat and make 'um a nice treacle puddin'. It would be a change from the kitchen maids legs I'd bin giving 'um.'

Seeing my questioning glance she said, good humouredly, 'Ent you ever heard of puddin' called kitchen maids legs before? They be boiled puddin's with currants in, what you calls a spotted dog!

'Well, I sent our Frankie, who was about nine at

the time, into the town to get this treacle. Just as 'e
got outside the gate the lad next door said to him,
"Wur bist goin' Frankie?" So 'e ses, "Down to
Painswick to buy a tin of traycle and if you comes
along wi' I, I'll let yu dip yer finger in." I ent never
fergot that', Nellie told me laughingly, 'Can you
imagine anybody walkin' all that way these days,
just to dip thur finger in a treacle tin eh?

'Our next move was to Gaginwell, that ent far
from here,' Nellie went on, 'Ah we stayed thur fer
about four years I think. I remembers one old dear
as lived next door to we said to I one day, "Missus
ull you come into Chippy with I, I got a bit of
shoppin' to do and I don't fancy goin' on me own,
I'll pay yer fare if you'll come."

'Well, I wasent goin' to turn a chance like that
down so off we goes. Her wanted to buy a new
mattress her said, her was fed up with the old
feather bed as her mother had given her.

'When we gets into Chippy her stalks straight
into the co-op furnishing. Up comes a smart young
fellow and asks her what 'er wants. "I wants a new
bed," 'er said, crackin' her jaw a bit.* I thought you
said as you wanted a mattress, I whispered to her.
"Ah so I do," 'er said, "Young man tis only a
mattress that I be hinterested in." So the young
man ses to her, "Yes madam, what sort? Do you
require a spring matress?". "Oh lorks no," 'er

* Putting her talk on

replied, "I don't want one just fer spring, he got to last I all the year round!"

'Talk about laugh, that poor fellow didn't know wur to put his face.'

Nellie rambled on with her tales, she was in good form this afternoon.

'Ah, and one farmer as my Harry worked for allus wore leather breeches—he used to have 'um made special like. Well one year they had a college bloke working on the farm durin' the summer holidays, and what ever he was doing, this yer young man always wore leather gloves. So the farmer ses to him one day, "Why do you always wear leather gloves at work my boy?" "To keep

my hands soft and white" he replied. "Well," the farmer said, "I've always worn leather breeches and you should see my backside, tis as brown as a berry!" '

SORTING SPUDS

The time passes very quickly as I listen to
Nellie's endless chatter. She comes from a large
family of eight boys and six girls. Her husband is
also one of a family of ten, so there are many
reminiscences and incidents to recall.

'We only had two bedrooms in our cottage, when
we was young and all the family was at home,' she
told me one day, 'so it was all the men and boys in
one room and we girls and our mother in the other,
twas the only way to be decent.

'And there was a fellow who lived next to us
who's name was Harry Bell, but we used to call
him "amorous Harry" cos he was a bit fast with
the girls, sort of fancied his-self he did. Mine you
he was goodlooking and nearly all the girls used to
chase after him. And if any new ones come to the
village I'll bet he was soon walkin' out with 'um.
He got that he'd brag summut awful about his con-
quests. So the village lads thought they'd play a
trick on him, and one of 'um offered to dress up as
a girl to see if he could get off with "amorous
Harry". Thur happened to be a penny hop in the
schoolroom on this particular night. Course thur
was no street lights in our village and twas as
black as pitch outside. Off goes "amorous Harry"
to the dance and as usual flirts with all the girls.
Then my brother goes up to him and said "Thur's
a smashing gal outside Harry, just up your strit,
why don't you come outside and meet her?" So

Harry, who was never backard at comin' forrod, was outside in a flash. He chatted this so-called "girl" up and then they went off down the lane with thur arms all round each other. And following close behind, unbeknown to Harry, was most of the lads. Well "amorous Harry" manoeuvres the "girl" up against a stile and he soon begins his overtures. Suddenly he starts swearin' and shoutin' at the top of his voice, "you be a man you bitch! you be a man you bitch!" Then he took to his heels and run off home.

'Well that taught him a lesson, he never did seem quite so amorous after that. As a matter of fact soon afterwards he settled down with one of the local girls, they got married and he turned out to be ever such a good husband and father.'

Just then two of Nellie's children came into the barn. We were working a bit later than usual to get an extra big load of potatoes done.

'Can we go flowerin' Mum?' they asked.

'Yes,' she replied, 'but don't get your feet wet. I know what they're after', she went on, 'they always likes to bring me the first violets. I heard their Dad tell 'um this mornin' that he could smell 'um, when he was down Mill Lane yesterday.'

Nellie and I had been picking out some smallish potatoes. I wanted to make some wheat and potato wine, which is very much like whiskey if its made properly. Harry said that he could supply me with

Nellie and *Harry* and *Family*

a pound of wheat, so on the whole it was going to be a very cheap gallon of wine. I promised to give them a bottle of it when it was fit. Nellie's didn't make wine, 'I ent got the time and I ent got the room,' she told me.

'Have you ever been down to the forest on Palm Sunday?' Nellie asked me one day.

'Forest,' I said, 'what forest?'

'Wychwood' she said, 'lots of people goes there on that day to visit the wells. Do you mean to stand there and say as you've never heard anything about it and you bin livin' in Oxfordshire all yer life!' Nellie cried.

'Well you see tis an old custom whats still kept up in the Wychwood forest and its called Spanish Sunday or Spanish Liquor day and it always falls on Palm Sunday. Tis the only day in the year that the public be allowed in the forest, unless you get a special permit fer bird watching and things like that. When we was kids we never missed goin', you see', she went on, 'we only lived three miles from thur and the night before we always got our bottles ready.'

'Bottles?' I asked.

'Yes, bottles,' she replied. 'That's the idea of going to the forest so that you can fill your bottle with the magic waters. Just before Spanish Sunday our mother would buy a piece of real black liquorice from an old lady in the village, she would chop it up and give us each a piece to put in our bottles, then along with that we'd put a spoonful of brown sugar and a black peppermint, and we'd hang our bottles up in the myrtle bush all Saturday night.'

'Why a myrtle bush?' I enquired.

'Well, that was to keep them safe from the witches,' she cried. 'The next morning we was up early and off we'd all go, gangs of us trailin' down to the forest. We had to walk about two miles before we got to the lakes or ponds, tha's what they calls the wells these days. And all along the grassy "rides" on the way to the wells there was little tiny springs, dozens of 'um all trickling down until they

fell into the lakes. When we reached the biggest
stretch of water, what the locals calls Lake Superior,
we dipped our bottles in and filled them up. Then
we'd shake the contents like billyho so as to mix it
all up. Then we'd drink this concoction and it was
supposed to cure anything that you had wrong with
you. Mind you,' Nellie went on, 'an old fellow told
I that hundreds of years ago somebody happened to
find out that this water from the forest contained a
lot of iron, and I suppose that was why folks started
drinkin' it. And I reckons that the liquorice and
sugar and sweets was added later, just to make it
taste better, though the liquorice was a sort of
medicine too. Mind you, that Spanish liquor always
had the same effect on I as young rhubarb do. I
don't think that many people bothers to take a bottle
with 'um these days, they can get all the medicine
they wants off the National Health. But I think its
a good thing that folks still goes down to the forest
on Spanish Liquor day, it'd be a pity if the custom
was dropped after all these years.

'Do you remember I told you that the general
public wasent allowed in the forest only on that
day?' Nellie said. 'Well that ent exactly true. You
see the people who lives in the villages that skirt
Wychwood forest still have whats called "wooding
rights" and they can go and pick up kindling wood
on certain afternoons, but you can only bring out
what you can carry in your arms because no wheeled

vehicles be allowed in thur, except of course of men who works in the forest, you know, clearin' the old wood and that sort of thing.'

I was fascinated by Nellie's information about Spanish Liquor day and promised myself that I'd not let another Palm Sunday slip by before I made a journey to the wells at Wychwood.

We finished the potato sorting about the third week in March. Nellie and I probably wouldn't meet again until the next potato harvest, although there was talk that the farmer might purchase a machine to gather up the crop, in which case none of the potato picking gang would be employed.

We were experiencing typical March weather, high racy winds. Someone told me once thats what they were for—'to blow away the last year's leaves and make way for the young un's to grow'. There certainly seemed to be a great spring cleaning of the land, the harrows were busy leaving the freshly planted fields flat and tidy. A wonderful month March, a forward looking month, with the wallflowers in bud and the crocus blooming bright and golden under the house wall. And although there may still be frosts and snow to come, spring can't be far away.

A Good Wheat and Potato Wine Recipe

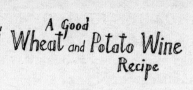

1 LB OLD POTATOES
1 LB WHEAT
1 LB PRUNES
1 GALLON WATER
3 LB DEMERARA SUGAR
1 OZ YEAST

Bring the water to the boil, take off heat and pour into a large crock or pan. Add potatoes that have been scrubbed and cut up small. Add sugar, wheat and chopped prunes. Stir well until the sugar has dissolved. When cool add the yeast which has been spread on to a piece of toast.

Leave for three or four days. When working has finished strain and carefully pour into a cask, jar or bottles, cork lightly until all working has finished, as transferring the wine from the pan to bottles often causes the wine to begin to work again. Leave for six months. Strain again through wine filters. This wine improves with keeping.

5

HOPPY THE ROADMAN

HOPPY the old roadman was one of the most fascinating characters in the village, and a conscientious hardworking man he was too. Keeping the roads tidy had not always been his job. For nearly forty-four years he had worked on one of the local farms; then one day, while they were threshing, he fell off a rick and that finished Hoppy's farm-working days.

After he got over breaking his hip he became the village roadman, and the place was richer for it. Almost anything the locals wanted to know, they asked Hoppy, and he nearly always had an answer for them.

He was a small, boney sort of man—'When I was a lad' he told me one day, 'I should have liked to have bin a jockey, but that would have meant going away to train, and our mother didn't want me to do that. So I started work when I was thirteen for farmer Harper and just stayed till I fell off the rick.'

He would often shout at me as I passed by on my bicycle—'I got a smashing little story for you my girl, come along at dinnertime and I'll tell you'. Hoppy knew I was collecting tales about country

people, and he had a store of them packed away in his lively mind. Some of the stories that he related to me were uproariously wonderful, but unprintable; and Hoppy told them with such feeling too.

For the story-telling episodes we usually sat on the vergeside, wherever Hoppy happened to be working. With our backs against a Cotswold wall and the larks singing above he would almost re-live incidents of the past.

There was the day when workmen had begun to demolish a row of derelict cottages in the village, and as we sat there lorries were passing by piled up with rubble and stone.

''Tis a shame knockin' they cottages down,' he said, 'I recons with a bit of money spent on 'um they'd a made good homes fer people. Course I can remember when they was proper smartish places, ah-h, you could rent one of 'um for three and six a week. I knows because we lived in one of 'um, when we was all at home; thirteen of us was brought up in that end cottage.

'And livin' next door to we was old Ben and Sarah Green, and they was allus quarrellin'. Nasty vicious quarrels they was too. If I'd a bin old Ben I should have left that old faggot Sarah years ago.

'I remembers one time when Ben had gone down to the Lion to 'ave a drink, and he hadn't bin down thur long when Sarah said as 'er was goin' down to drag 'im out.

'Well, down the village 'er stalks, and into the Lion. "Come on 'ome you wicked old beggar", 'er shouted to him, "wastin' yer time and money in yer." And to Sarah's surprise, instead of swearin' back at 'er old Ben said, "Righto me old wench, I be comin', I be just awf out the back—shan't be a couple of minutes."

'After waitin' for about a quarter of an hour Sarah ses to old Charlie, 'e as keeps the Lion, "You'd best go and see wur 'e's got to. He might 'ave 'ad an accident or summut, fell down your old lavartory I shouldn't wonder." But old Ben had gone out the back way and 'ad 'urried off 'ome— just to 'ave 'er one. And by the time Sarah 'ad got back, he'd gone to bed and he'd locked 'er out.

''Er banged on the door fer ages, but old Ben never took no notice. Then 'er got the clothes prop and tapped the bedroom window. After a bit Ben comes to the window, pokes 'is 'ead out an' ses, "What do you want now, you wicked old varmit?"

' "Don't ask such daft questions you silly old beggar" old Sarah shouted to him, "you come down an' let I in."

' "Oh no," Ben ses. "I don't encourage folks to be out all hours lolloping outside public houses. You go and sleep in the out-house, same as I've 'ad to affor now".

'Later on that same year old Ben was took bad, that bad as Sarah called in the doctor.

' "Well, what do you think of 'im?" 'er asked the Doctor as he come down the stairs.

' "He's a very sick man Mrs. Green. If he's got any relations you'd better send for them, he won't last long," the doctor told 'er.

'A couple of days arter this, old Ben took a turn for the worst, but old Sarah left 'im alone, 'er was busyin' herself about the house—there'd be 'er

brother Tom a-comin' and that dragon of a sister of old Ben's, Clara, and 'er husband Sid, 'e as ate like a pig, and they'd want to stay overnight.

'Well, later on that afternoon Sarah 'eard Ben

tappin' faintly on the floor with 'is walkin' stick, 'er went to the stairs door and shouted, "What do you want now then?"

'Old Ben called down in a weak voice, "Is that a bit of 'ome cured 'am you be cookin' Sarah?"

' "And what of it?" 'er ses to 'im, nasty like.

' "Well that do smell good, I fancies a bit 'a that fer me tea." Back come old Sarah's voice, as sharp as a knife, "Thee get on with thee dyin' you wicked old beggar, that 'ams fer thee funeral."

'And do you know,' Hoppy went on, ''er never shed a tear when old Ben died a couple a days later. Still 'er didn't enjoy 'er widowhood long. One night about a month arter, Sarah went out into the garden to draw up a bucket a water from the well, and folks recons that just as 'er bent over a gust of wind must 'ave lifted 'er off 'er feet and 'er went head fust down the well.

'When postman Townsend called with a letter in the mornin', he found the door open, but nobody about; 'e searched about a bit, then looked down the well and thur 'er was. Providence, tha's what our mother said it was.'

Hoppy took out his watch, 'we just got time fer another,' he said, 'I'll tell you one tha's a bit more cheerful, tis about one a the cricket matches that we use to 'ave in the village years ago. My word, we had some humdingers then.

'Ah-h once every summer we played a damned

good match with a team from Crowsbottom; you know the place, about six miles from yer, and the prize fer the winnin' side was a five gallon barrel of beer. And although twas a friendly match, each side allus done thur best to win—and the ones that did sort of felt as they was top dogs.

'Mind you,' Hoppy went on, 'the field was a bit on the rough side wur we played. The night affor this match as I be tellin' you of, old Jim Banks had got 'is herd a cows in thur and that old cricket pitch was fair smamsed up wi' cow muck. And some of the players finished up wi' more of it on thur clothes than thur was on the grass. But nobody minded, it all made a bit of fun with everybody takin' it in thur stride.

'Well, our fellows gets that Crowsbottom lot out fer sixty-eight, and they was certain that they could beat that score. But things didn't go too well, the fust seven of our chaps was out fer thirty. Then Bert Makepeace goes out to bat and 'e looked like stayin' fer ever. All we villagers was a cheerin' 'im on as 'e slashed away knockin' the ball for four, time and time agen. Ah-h and 'e made thirty-three affor 'e was caught out.

'That only left Hurdle Weaver, Smag Holly and Old Shackutts, and none of um 'ad ever scored no more than 'alf a dozen between um.

'Fust Hurdle goes out to bat—full of 'is self 'e was, but 'e was soon back agen, out fer a duck as usual. That left Smag and Shackutts to hold the fort. And our fellows begun to think as that barrel a beer was already gone to t'other side.

'Down comes the ball towards Shackutts like a bullet out of a gun and everybody 'eld thur breath a-waitin' fer the stumps to be knocked clean out of thur 'oles. But to the crowd's surprise old Shackutts hit that ball hard and sent it over the field—it bounced on the ground then shot straight up the spout of farmer Banks pump—you know one a they old lead pumps what folks used to pump thur water up from the wells with.

'That ball was stuck firm up the spout, one and another tried to get it down and all the time Shackutts and Smag was runnin' backwards and forwards, red-faced and sweatin' and the crowd a-cheerin' um on. Course they got thur six runs, long affor somebody got that old ball down.

'All our team ran out on the field, they picked up the barrel of beer then they set old Shackutts on the top of it and carried 'im off as if they was carrying the World Cup. My word didn't we all celebrate—I reckons as half the village was drunk that night. We drunk the pub dry and the landlord's wife finished up the night by givin' us gallons of 'er home-made wine.

'They carried old Shackutts 'ome at closin' time—drunk as a lord 'e was—hero of the day he'd bin, and the villagers never forgot it.'

Hoppy packed up his flask and paper into his dinner bag and hung it on his bike handles.

'I be goin' to do a bit a scythin' this arternoon' he said, knowing I should want to stop and watch for a while.

He sharpened the huge curved blade with a grey-blue sharpening stone and then started to cut the verge-sides. It looked so easy, that slow steady sweep that he took, as he felled the swaying grasses, moon daisies and blue cranesbill.

I had tried my hand at scything once, but, as Hoppy said, 'It takes a bit of gettin' used to.'

Hoppy came to a patch of purple thistles, 'Dang nusaince, tha's all thistles be, I should 'ave cut 'um affor this' he said, taking a mighty sweep at the five-foot tall weeds. 'Do you know that little rhyme about these blessed things' he went on, wiping the sweat from his ruddy face.

> *Cut 'um in May they'll spoil yer hay,*
> *Cut 'um in June 'tis a bit too soon,*
> *Cut 'um in July, then 'um ull die.*

'Course I suppose that saying's for farmers, not for roadmen; ah I should have cut 'um weeks ago,' Hoppy said.

I left him scything away, taking long, steady sweeps at the weeds with his newly sharpened blade. I had some shopping to do in the town but promised I'd stop and have another chat with him on my way back. I knew that he had a break for a cup of tea at about three o'clock.

The wonderful smell of fresh cut grass met me when I returned. I was amazed to see the amount of ground that Hoppy had covered. All along the verge-side layers of thistles and grasses lay wilting in the hot afternoon sun. I noticed that he had left some of the wild flowers growing—I stood watching him, skimming round a clump of blue cranes-bill, he cut very close to them but not one fell under the sharp blade.

'I 'ent got the heart to cut 'um all down,' he said, looking at me, 'they be such a lovely colour, when they be full out.

'I found summut as I knows you'd like to see,' he went on, 'come and have a look at this little nest.' I followed him to a clump of blackberry bushes. There, suspended between two bramble sprays was the loveliest little nest, beautifully made of bits of dried grass and lined with horse-hair, in it snug and warm lay five green speckled eggs, awaiting the miracle of birth.

'I wonder how many journeys they little birds had to make before they had enough stuff to build that nest,' Hoppy said. 'Listen, can't you hear they birds a-scolding us because we be near their home.'

The pair were flitting about from bush to bush twittering and chattering trying to entice us away from the nest.

'Billy Whitethroats they be,' he went on, 'I allus knows summer's here when they arrives. Keeps me eye open for 'um I do, then suddenly one morning I sees 'um in the hedge, they seems to come back year after year to the very same place.'

As we walked away from the bramble bush the scolding died down and was soon lost in the hot afternoon air.

The scorching sun had dried the swathes of grass which Hoppy had cut earlier in the day into sweet smelling hay; he kicked at the layers with his foot. 'Ah, and thur it'll stay till it all disappears I suppose,' he said, 'and yets I minds the time when small farmers have bin glad to come along and gather all this verge-side hay up, and some of 'um used to let the cows graze the sides of the roads too, on thur way to and from milking.

'I'll tell 'e what my girl,' he went on, 'there don't seem many frogs about this year. As a rule when I be scything they little beggers be hopping about like mad things in the grass. No, I can't say as I've seen more than half a dozen this summer. 'Tis all that spray tackle whats killing 'um off, it 'ent natural fer animals to be destroyed like it—they 'ull be having a go at we next,' he said laughingly.

'Ah, I suppose that old Cuckoo 'ull be going back any day now—I ent heard him calling for a day or so now. 'Tis funny, all winter we longs to hear him and before you knows where you be, they be all gone back to Africa.

'Thurs a good bush of Elderflowers over in that field,' Hoppy said, inclining his head. 'You don't want to pick 'um from the side of the road if you can help it, they got too much dust on 'um.'

I promised to come and gather some the next day, when I hadn't any shopping to carry. You must gather Elderflowers just at the right time for wine making—not with any of the flowers still in bud, for that will make the wine taste bitter, and not with any of the tiny flowerets falling or that will make the wine taste like Elderflowers smell, which is not very pleasant. I make both Elderflower wine and Champagne, the latter can be drunk two weeks after making and is the loveliest most refreshing drink imaginable, and a great favourite of ours.

During the night we had a heavy thunderstorm so I waited a couple of days before setting out to gather the Elderflowers. You must also pick them when they are dry and with the sun shining on them if possible.

Hoppy had moved a couple of miles further down the road. 'To another part of me *length*' as he calls the four or five miles of roadway that he has to keep clean and tidy. As usual he was pleased to see me.

'You knows the right time to come don't you my gel,' he said jokingly, 'I was thinking twas time I stopped fer me afternoon drink. I reckoned as how you'd be coming today, so I left enough fer us both to have a mouthful.

'We'd best set on the wall today,' Hoppy went on, 'that grass still strikes up a bit damp. My word, that didn't stop to rain did it? All I've done since is clean out they little gullies—you know the little channels what I digs in the verge-sides so that the water will drain off the road. They was all blocked up with hay and rubbish. It's funny', he said, 'that I should be ending me days as a roadman, for my old father done the same job for the last seven years of his working life. Mind you, conditions be a lot better than they was in his time, at least we got fairly good road surfaces these days. I've heard him say that 'twas nothing but dirt and stones then. And one of his most useful tools was a mud scraper —ah a bit wider than a garden rake it was. Course with all the horses and carts a-coming off the fields and they dirt roads, you can imagine how clapered up they'd get after a storm. Well he used to scrape this yer mud off the roads and pile it up on the grass. And after a bit, that dried and powdered down very fine. And during his dinnertime he used to sift this dirt and sell it to the local builders for 1s. 6d. a cart-load. I suppose they used it to mix along with summut else for building purposes. And another way he earned a bit extra was by selling beech leaves, fer compost. You see thur was quite

a big beech wood along the road where he'd got his "length". Well one of the farmer's wives from the next village was a very keen gardener, and every week in the autumn-time her 'ud bring two or three sacks and drop 'um off on her way to market. And my dad would get 'um filled up ready for her to collect on her way home. Ah, he used to get 3d. a bag fer they. Threepence don't seem much these days, but I'll bet that was as good as a five shilling piece to my father.'

Just at that moment a dog fox slipped quickly and quietly over the wall about two hundred yards up the road from where we were sitting. He crossed the road and was over the field before we could get our breath.

'Crikey,' Hoppy cried, getting up to start work again, 'he's damned hungry, or his family is, fer him to be out at this time of day. I'll bet he's got his lair in that old quarry over at Westfields. Have you ever seen fox-cubs at play? Lovely they be to watch, pity they has to grow up to be so destructive. I remembers once when I worked on a farm, my gaffer had got a broody hen sitting on some ducks' eggs, her 'ad been set thur about a couple of weeks and one morning he went to feed 'er and thur 'er was set thur with no yead, a fox 'ad et it off, and that wasn't all, 'e ad bit the yeads off six of his pullets too. 'Twas his own fault really, 'twas too much trouble to go and shut 'um up at nights.

Course he took perticler notice to shut 'um up arter that.'

Hoppy kicked over a freshly made mole-hill on the verge-side, 'Busy little beggars ent they,' he said, 'when I was a youngster I used to set traps to catch 'um. I used to get 6d. a skin for 'um, but nobody seems to bother to catch 'um these days. Ah, and talking about traps, have you ever sin one a they awful man-traps? Poachers' Penalty they was nicknamed. Terrible things they was, break a man's leg if he happened to get caught in one. Course they never bin used in my time, but I knows where there is one—still in the wood wur he was set all they years ago, and do you know my gel, he's all tangled up in the branches of a big beech tree, it just grew through the iron work I suppose. I expect when they used it, that there beech tree was just a sapling.

'Not that you can compare a mole trap with a man-trap or a gin trap fer that matter,' Hoppy said, 'but seeing that molehill reminded I to tell you about it.'

'I remember seeing a man-trap hung up in the yard of the Bull Hotel at Burford,' I said to him. And as I rode home I thought of another poaching tale that one of my old pals had told me, but that will have to wait for another day. Now my one thought was the Elderflowers that needed picking over, ready to make wine and Champagne.

Sarah Cook's Elderflower Champagne

2 HEADS OF ELDERFLOWERS
1½ LB WHITE SUGAR
1 GALLON OF WATER
2 TABLESPOONS OF WHITE-WINE VINEGAR
1 LEMON

Pick the heads when in full bloom. Take off any green stems however small. Put the blossoms into a bowl, sprinkle over the juice from the lemon, grate the rind and add this along with the sugar and vinegar. Add the cold water and leave for twenty-four hours. Strain into bottles and cork firmly and lay the bottles on their sides. Do not disturb for two weeks when the champagne should be sparkling and ready to drink. Do not try and keep this drink, as you would wine.

MISSUS-NEXT-DOOR

MIDSUMMER DAY had come and gone
before I had the chance to visit Mark again.
It was one of those perfect June days—the grass
verges were waist high with (Kek) Cow parsley,
Moon Daisies and Hemlock, and in the fields huge
red balers thumped out hay bales at an alarming
rate, and following in their wake sunburned men
who loaded them on to trailers. Cattle stood under
the trees idly flicking flies from their warm, pink
bodies, and there wasn't a cloud in the china blue sky.

I made for the hamlet where Mark lived; he was
having a few days holiday after almost three hectic
weeks of sheep shearing. His first words to me were:

'You'll never guess wass goin' to 'appen to we—
we be movin'.'

For a moment I hardly believed it, then he went
on, 'You needn't look so surprised, my wench—I
byen't going far—only up to the top end of the
village.'

'But why?' I protested, 'I thought you loved your
little old cottage. And what about the garden?', I
added, knowing that his tidy plot was his pride and
joy.

'Well you see 'tis like this, you can blame it all

on to that operation I had. You knaw that little
district Nuss that used to come in an' 'ave a look
at I—arter I'd 'ad me stitches out? Well, 'er must
'ave reported what conditions we lived under—used
to go on summut dreadful about ower cottage—and
last sprintime Missus-next-door 'ad a fall, an' that
same Nuss used to come an' see 'er—an' 'er told
Missus-next-door as 'er'd complain to the Council
about fetchin' water from the garden and trapesin'
all down that garden path to they lavatories—and
that rain comin' in, you 'as to set in thur with a
umberala up when thas rainin'.

'We only heard about it yes'day. Good job
Gaffer got they two cottages empty up the top end
—they used to be used fer the cowman and fer one
a the tractor drivers, but they both got such gret
families they bin moved up to the Council 'ouses.
Mind you they cottages bin done up—they recons
they be nice, cosy little places now.'

We were sitting outside Mark's cottage, the
garden was ablaze with colour and summer glory,
there were masses of flowers everywhere. Over the
walls trailed honeysuckle and roses, and cushions of
pinks and pansies spilled over the flagstoned path.

Poor old Mark—having to leave this—he and
his brother had lived here for nearly thirty years. I
had seen the cottages 'up the top end'. They had
been vacant for almost a year and the gardens were
waist high in nettles and docks.

'Ah-h but 'tis only temp'rey, just while they be doing ower cottage up', old Mark said, almost as if he was reading my thoughts. 'We shall be back yer in about six months—well, tha's what they ses— but you knaws what they builder chaps be, keeps

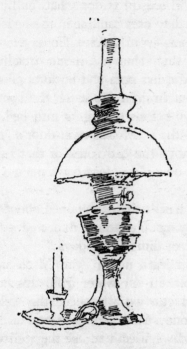

knockin' awf fer tea they do, like as not tu'll be a twelvemonth affor we be back. Course, we knawed as 'ow they was condemned years ago, and Missus-next-door 'er was born in 'er cottage—and 'er's goin' on fer sixty-five and thur en't bin a darn thing done to um since 'er bin married and tha's farty years ago.

'We 'ave got the 'lectric mind you, but Missus-next-door 'er got none, a paraffin stove 'er cooks by in summer, and that old fire oven in winter, and 'er still got the old oil lamps what 'er lights of a night; course they uses candles in the bedrooms.

'And 'er roof—you can see from yer, 'es in a terrible state, that rains in summut dreadful in the bedrooms, and thurs pots and buckuts all over the place when tha's rainin', to catch the spots—ah-h and sometimes before they gets into bed, 'er and old Charlie—tha's Missus-next-door's husband, they has tu move the bed round if that rain starts comin' in in a new place, leastways tha's what they tells we.'

'Why ever hasn't she complained about the conditions, surely people aren't expected to put up with that sort of thing these days?'

'You 'aven't 'eard nothin' yet' Mark said. 'We still 'as to fetch all our water from this tap in the garden—mind you we allus used the well water, then one day one a they sanitation men come pokin' round and said we wasn't to use the well water no more. And they put us this tap in and now we 'as the water from the main—leastways tha's what they thinks, but ower Fred and me we often 'as a drop of water from this yer well—thur's nothin' sweeter nor clearer than well water, though mind you in summer we do get newts in thur. But they little beggers don't 'urt—we chucks 'um back in again. I recon's everythings sent fer a purpose— p'rhaps they newts etts summat in that water as might do we some harm.

'Course tha's another thing the sanitation man said 'e 'ud get done, that lavatory of owern, but I recons they fergot all about it. Tha's the place— that little old stwon buildin' at the bottom of the garden.' From where I was sitting I could see the tumbledown 'little house'.

Mark went on, 'Now if I thinks a minute I shall remember just what that sanitation man said about it.' And he pushed his cap on to the back of his head and scratched his thick white hair.

'Ah-h, now I remembers—'e said 'twas a dreadful little 'ole—'e wants to pay we a call when I be emptin' 'im sometimes, 'e 'ud think as twas a dreadful little 'ole all right. All 'e done was just poke 'is yed round the door—and that was enough fer 'im. I suppose 'e was one of they town chaps what be used to they water closets. But we dun't take no notice, we be used to 'um.

'But we be lucky really, we 'ave got an old sink in ower 'ouse—mind you thur yent no 'ole fer the water tu run away, we brings it outside an' chucks it down the drain. But Missus-next-door 'ent got a sink to stand a bowl in—'er's a lot worse off than we really.

'And every time you 'as a bath you 'as tu fetch that old tin bath in—'e 'as 'angs up thur on the wall —then you lights a fire in the old wash-house copper, and when that water is nice and hot—thur you 'as tu sit—a stack a' coal on one side and a great bundle of faggots on 'tother—an' in winter the wind whistles under that old door—that east wind just sets in thur. I tells 'e, I don't 'ave no more baths than I be obliged to, that 'ud give I the pnemonia quicker than anything I recons.

'Course, it'll be all so different when they've done these cottages up, they be goin' to take all the stwon flags up in the kitchen, an' put a decent floor down. And when they've put a new roof on, Missus-next-door won't know what to do with all 'er pots and buckuts what 'er got up in the bedroom.'

'Is she looking forward to an easily run home', I asked, 'or would she rather jog along as she's going now?'

'Well, 'er recons that 'er won't knaw what to do with 'erself all day—you see thur won't be any stwon floors to scrub—no oil lamps tu clean and

fill—no runnin' in and out with bowls and buckuts of water—and no more standin' in that freezin' cold wash-house to do 'er washin'.

'Old Charly 'ave offered to buy 'er one a they washin' machines, but I thinks 'ers too old in the yead to start using one a they contraptions.'

Just then Mark's neighbour, Missus-next-door came out. She had laid a tray with pretty rose-covered china—her best I should think, and several chunks of home-made cake—seedy, raisin and fruit.

'I thought you'd like a drop of tay, 'tis a thursty sort of day. Well if you bent thursty,' she said, looking at me, 'I knaws 'e is, for 'e chatters that much as 'e can't 'ave got a bit of spittle left in 'is mouth. Did 'e tell 'e as we got to move—fancy havin' to shift at my time of life—like rootin' up one a they old elm trees. Come and see I affor you goes', she called to me over her shoulder, 'I got one or two little orniments as I think you'll like; 'e says you be fond of little curios.'

I thanked her then—and again when she gave me two blue 'vawses' as she called them, lovely delicate china they were.

'You really shouldn't give me these—they might be quite valuable,' I said.

'Never mind about that, I might break 'um when we moves—I'd much rather think you had got 'um safe in your house. I knows as you'll look after 'um fer 'e ses you got quite a little collection. Perhaps movin' out of this yer hollow might do I a bit of good', she went on, 'fer I've 'ad the yeadache fer that long I fergets what its like not to have one.'

'What does the doctor say, or haven't you been to see him?' I enquired.

'Oh bless me soul I've bin to see him many a time, he have put it down to all sorts of things; now 'e ses that its me tith whats causin' me yead to ache so. 'E ses to I one day—Mrs Hawkins 'e ses, if you was to 'ave your tith out you'd 'ave no more yeadaches. So I ses to 'im, Doctor, if you think thats what 'tis I'll 'ave 'um all out—though what in the name of wonderment me yeads got to do with me tith I don't know.

'Well, I 'ad 'um all out, proper goormless I looked too, and I with me mouth as empty as a new born babe.

'Then come the time fer I to go and 'ave me pressure took. All that chap kept doin' was to keep puttin' a gret lump of 'ot putty in me mouth, made I as sick as a dog it did. So I ses to 'im after 'e 'ad bin muckin' about with me poor mouth fer about half an hour, "Look yer young man, if its all the same to you I won't 'ave no artificials—never thought 'twas all thus fuss and bother. I've 'ad the yeadache fer forty years and I recons I can put up with it fer a bit longer."

'Then the doctor said that it might be me stummuck. So I ses to 'im, 'old 'ard doctor, if you thinks I be goin' to 'ave me stummuck out you got another think. I byent 'alf the woman I was before I 'ad me tith out. Lord knows what I should look like with me stummuck out as well.

'Oh 'e did laugh, but 'e still thinks as I ought to persevere and 'ave some artificials, although they do say 'tis like walking about with a mouthful of gravestwons.'

I bade her goodbye and hoped that both she and Mark would be settled in the cottages up the top end of the village by the next time I came to visit.

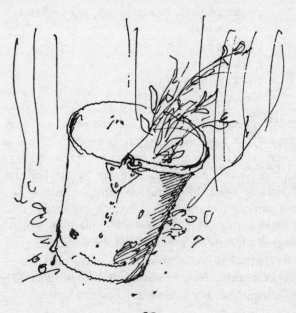

Doris Bracknell's Elderflower Wine

3 PINTS OF ELDERFLOWERS
(measure them in a pint cup, jug or basin)
3 LB SUGAR
2 LEMONS
2 ORANGES
1 GALLON WATER
½ OZ YEAST

Pick all green stalks from Elderflowers, place in a saucepan and cover with water, bring to the boil and simmer for fifteen minutes. Add the sugar and the rind from the lemons and oranges, bring to the boil again and simmer again for a further fifteen minutes. Strain into a pan and add the juice of lemons and oranges. Mix the yeast with a drop of warm wine, place on a piece of toast and slip this on to the top of the wine. Leave until all fermentation has ceased, then bottle and leave at least six months. Now strain through paper wine filters —this will clear any sediment.

7

COTSWOLD FRIENDS

THE first two weeks in July had been dull and wet, but at last the weather had changed for the better. The sun shone on the ripening corn, turning the landscape to the colour of a lion. This is 'between time'—the hay harvest and silage cutting is over—the corn, not quite ripe, stands waiting motionless, the bustling days of harvest are yet to come.

I was off to visit my old friends Ethel and Fred Atkins. I'd had a card from them days ago reminding me of a long promised visit, coupled with the fact that Ethel had written 'we be just got into a nice bit of pigmeat'.

I pushed my bike up a steep hill; there was wild thyme growing by the dusty roadside and here and there the verges were blue with drifts of meadow cranesbill, and fat brown bumble bees flew drunkenly about in the sleepy summer haze.

I zoomed down into the valley and passed over a humped-back bridge, underneath which a gentle stream trickled and sang. At the water's edge large patches of purple loosestrife stood straight and soldierly. And by the old stone bridge a little group of wide-eyed, pink-faced children dawdled, their

arms filled with jam-jars and fishing nets. In some of the cottage gardens lace curtains had been draped over ripening currants and raspberries, in a vain attempt to keep the yellow billed blackbirds at bay.

Ethel and Fred were waiting for me; I was given such a royal welcome. Going into their house was like entering a miniature jungle, plants clambered up, hung down, wandered and sprawled over window sills and ledges. Licking tongues of cacti caught your sleeve, drawing you into the steamy jungle. Pots of geraniums were packed closely on side tables and shelves, and amongst it all Ethel and

Fred sat like a pair of bright-eyed, red-faced gnomes.

'We be glad you be come,' Ethel said, ''E bin talkin' of nothin' else fer days, and we be got into the nicest bit of pigmeat as you ever taisted. And Fred was up that early this mornin',' she burbled on, 'you see my dear, we be goin' to have our own new taters today, first of the season, and he've picked some a they green winsors, 'e ses they be just fit, we knows as you loves a few broad beans boiled in the bacon water; thur yent nothin' nicer nowhere than that. Lorks 'ow I do go on,' she cried, 'yer be I a-chatterin' and I ent even put the kettle on.' She scuttled out to the back scullery still chattering.

'We be goin' to have you all to ourselves for the rest of the day,' she said excitedly. 'My Fred said to I this mornin', "Missus" 'e said, "by eight o'clock tonight that old tongue of yourn 'ull be fit to drop out, dang me if 'e wont."'

We wandered out into the beautiful garden. 'You be just come right,' Fred said, as he proudly showed me round. 'That won't never look no better than it do now.'

Every flower that ever grew in a summer garden was blooming there; the long border was a blaze of colour and there wasn't a weed in sight. Beyond the rustic fence, where Clematis, Honeysuckle and Roses tumbled, was a splendid vegetable garden.

'Plenty of pig muck, thas what makes the tackle grow,' Fred told me when I complimented him on his wonderful crops. 'Come and have a look at our youngsters,' he went on, and we made our way to the top of the garden where two young pink pigs grunted happily.

'They byent very old but they be doin' nicely,' he said, scratching the backs of the animals. 'You got to make a fuss of 'um, pigs loves a bit of fuss—they thrives on it!'

Arms folded we leaned on the top rail of the pig run. It was built just the right height for this pleasant pastime—no words were necessary—we just leaned and gazed—gazed and leaned, while the pigs greedily ate the cabbage leaves that Fred had thrown to them.

'Well mother,' he said turning to his wife, 'its about time that dinner was done, I be fair famished.'

'By the time we gets down home it'll all be just ready to "strain up",' she answered happily.

We entered the cool kitchen. Ethel had laid the table with her best linen. She had placed a bowl of gloriously coloured sweet peas in the centre and their delicate smell filled the room.

The meal was first class; the bacon was done to a turn and the young potatoes and broad beans simply melted in our mouths. Raspberries, freshly gathered that morning and made into a delicious tart, swilled down with Ethel's Elderflower champagne, completed a wonderful meal. We moved out into the garden.

Here was all the peace and quiet that anyone ever wished for. Ethel and Fred had lived here for over forty years, they were happy and contented and loved every stick and stone. The words of Amos Alcott came into my mind: 'Who loves a garden, still his Eden keeps'.

The unmistakable smell of jam-making floated over the privet hedge. 'That's my neighbour,' Ethel explained, 'her said her was a-goin' jam-makin' this afternoon. I've made quite a lot meself: raspberry, blackcurrant, and his favourite gooseberry', she nodded in the direction of Fred's sleeping form. 'I don't really make jam with me raspberries,' she went on, 'its called "preserve", and you don't have to boil it, and it tastes just like the fresh fruit. And its a lovely colour too. I'll give 'e the recipe, if you'd like it. Once you've made it this way you'll never make ordinary jam again. Then I makes home-made wine with all the tail-end fruits, thas what I calls me mixed-fruit wine—thas nice and sweet, and course its a lovely colour too. Fred's favourite that is,' Ethel said proudly.

'I remembers that was my father's favourite too. He was head keeper at Catsford Park. Did I ever tell you about the time 'e got shot?' she went on, not waiting for my answer. 'I was about eleven at the time and our Mother was expecting a baby and because she was near her time I was allowed to stay up to keep her company while my father went out to try and catch some poachers. You see he had been losing a lot of pheasants, and fer the past week 'e'd bin going back to the spinneys at night-time to see if he could catch the thieves. Well about two o'clock in the morning he comes staggering in—he'd bin shot in the arm and another bullet had grazed his leg. And when he took his hat off, there was a bullet hole right through the top. If that had bin two inches lower he'd never bin alive to tell the tale. You see, keepers used to wear brown hard hats something like a bowler only higher in the crown. Well, as soon as it was daylight I was sent off with a note for the doctor. Mind you our Dad only had about four days off from work. And he never did find out who took a pot shot at him that night.

'Anyhow, about thirty years after the shooting a very peculiar thing happened. By then my father had died—nothing to do with the shooting mind you, no, I thinks twas pneumonia what took him off in the end. Well, my mother was still living in the same cottage, and we girls had married and left home. One day there was a knock at the door, and a big smartly-dressed middle-aged man stood there, brown as a berry he was. Then he ses to our mother "Mrs. Hackett isent it?" sort of talking down his nose.

'Yes, I'm Mrs. Hackett' her said.

'Then this man blurted out, "Mrs. Hackett I've come home to confess". Our mother sort of thought that her ought to know who it was, so her asks him indoors. Then he blurts out again, "I've come back to confess, all these years and I've never forgot that night when I killed your husband."

'Then our mother realised who it was. Twas Jack Arnott who used to live over at Little Cowpens. And this was the man who had shot my father. At the time they thought that he might have been the poacher, but nobody could find out where he'd gone. Some said as he might have joined the army, but nobody was sure. He was never heard of again until the day he knocked at our mother's door.

'Talk about relieved when he learned that my

father didn't die on that night over thirty years ago.

'Course then our mother had to hear the full story. How this 'ere Jack Arnott took aim and he knew that he'd hit my father, cos he went down like a log, and when he didn't get up and chase him well he was proper scared. So Jack took to his heels and run and run—all through the night. He slept in hayricks and sheds, only moving after it was dark until he got to Cardiff, wur he joined a ship and in time he got to Australia. He'd got on ever so well, a respectable married man he was. But he just had to come back and make his peace. All they years of worrying, and all fer nothing. Still,' Ethel went on, 'you couldn't help but admire the fellow fer coming back as soon as he could afford it. Anyhow he went back home a very happy man. After that he always kept in touch with our mother—and each Christmas he sent her a big parcel, filled with tinned foods of every sort.'

Fred began snoring loudly. 'Hark at him,' Ethel said, 'he bin that busy getting it all to look nice fer your visit, now I suppose he thinks as how he can relax a bit. A cup of tea, that'll wake him I'll be bound,' she cried, and she scuttled indoors to put the kettle on.

The scents from the flowers—pinks, stocks and roses—wafted across to where we were sitting, and the peaceful afternoon wore on.

'I'll tell you about another man who lived in our

village,' Ethel said after we'd settled down again. Sid Thomas his name was, and he was the local sweep. Ah, he'd sweep my mother's chimney fer the top of a cottage loaf.'

'For the top of a loaf?' I queried.

'Ah, like as not her hadn't got no money in the house. Folks was so hard up in them days. I can remember when the village cobbler would sole yer boots fer a whole loaf and he'd do it while you waited. And women used to go out and get black-berries and walk into Oxford and sell em for 2d a lb to the jam factories.

'Still I was a-telling you about the sweep fust go awf. He was such a kind man, all we kids loved old Sid, nobody called him Mr., not even we children. He'd got a lovely donkey that pulled a little trap, and after he'd finished his chimney sweepin' he'd take a few of us children for a ride round the village. Mind you we had to take something to give the donkey to eat, sort of payment for the ride. We would cadge carrots or apples, or perhaps a bit of bran from our mother. And once,' she went on, 'he took us all round Faketon Hall park, that was about three miles out of the village. It must have been about 1909, and some sort of royal event, corona-tion or something special, anyhow he gave us little Union Jacks to wave as we jogged along in his trap.

'Ah, an' once he went to prison—for assaultin' a

policeman. Mind you he used to get terrible drunk. He was the night he was arrested. But he was such a well-loved man that a lady, and I mean a real educated lady, paid for the hay for his donkey all the time he was in prison. And another time when thur was a general election on, he painted his doorstep and his donkey and trap bright blue, just to let the people know who he was a-voting for. He tore round and round the village shoutin' and hollerin' politics at the top of his voice; course he was drunk as usual. The police tried to catch him, but he just managed to stumble indoors so they couldn't arrest him. He used to tell everybody that when he died he didn't want anybody to grieve and that he wanted a band to play at his funeral, and they was to play cheerful music. The day he was laid to rest a brass band come over from the next village and they played all old Sid's favourite songs, what he used to sing in the pubs. The folks was a-cryin' and singin' at the same time. We kids even had a day off from school. And Sid's wife and two sons followed in his trap with his faithful old donkey in the shafts. Ah, 'e certainly was a nice fellow, I don't think thur was anybody who'd say a bad word against him, except the police.

'Mind you, the village was a rough old place at that time. One old man used to tell us that just fer a bit of excitement on a Saturday night, he and some of the other young fellows would take off their jackets and dangle 'um in front of the pub windows. This was a challenge to anybody inside to come out and have a fight with 'um. Dreadful place it was fer fightin', it was. Still I suppose they had to liven up the village a bit and that was the only way they knew.

'Ah, an' long before my time thur used to be a witch in our village—well so my old granny used to tell I. Mind you, over the years I expect the story have got exaggerated a bit, but I do recall her a-tellin' about this perticler one.

'Saleena they used to call her; mind you her was quite clever really, 'er could cure all sorts of things. But 'er could be very nasty if folks upset her. Well, there was this big bully who used to tease 'er and say as 'er hadn't got no magic. Once or twice 'er threatened him and said as 'ow 'er would cast a spell on him if he kept on. Well one day in the street he started on 'er again, so 'er ses to him "George James, I've warned you affor, and now I means it, I be goin' to put a curse on you that'll last till you die or I die. You shall dance along the rooftops every time thurs a full moon and nothin' on earth 'ull stop you."

'Well 'e goes swaggerin' off down the street sayin' as twas a lot of poppycock, but sure enough come the next full moon thur 'e was up thur a-dancin' along the thatched roofs of all the cottages. So when the next full moon was due 'e got some of

the menfolk to tie him down with big strong ropes, so as he shouldn't go runnin' around again. But long before midnight thur 'e was a-dancin' about on the roofs again. This went on fer quite a long time and poor old George got that thin and bad, with worry. So some of the village men planned to catch old Saleena and try to kill 'er. But twas easier said than done. Witches be funny things to try and kill. Well they caught her and eight of 'um held her down in the pond to try and drown 'er, that took 'um four hours before 'er was really dead. Then they had to find somewhere to bury 'er; you see you can't bury a witch on consecrated ground. So they takes her out of the village to what was called Highwayman's Corner; twas a little three-cornered piece of grass at the crossroads. They digs a grave and buried her there and soon old George James was his old self again, no more runnin' about on the roofs at full moon. But yers the funny bit, and I knows its true cost I've seen it. That three-cornered piece of grass wur they buried old Saleena is still thur, and right in the middle of it thurs a strip what measures two feet wide by five feet long whats never had no grass on!'

'Tis true,' Fred said, seeing my unbelieving glance, 'I've seen it meself, but don't you ask neither of us wur tis cos we shan't tell you, cos that would bring us bad luck. But now you knows the story you just keep your eyes open for it and perhaps one day you'll come across it, like we did. I expect you've passed the spot dozens of times, but didn't think anything about it.'

The sun had left the garden, and for a moment I felt a shiver run down my back. Ethel noticed it. 'Come on my dear,' she said, 'don't take too much notice of what we tells you.' But the story intrigued me and I vowed to look for the bare patch two feet wide by five feet long on a green triangle—somewhere in the county.

There was a bag of 'they winsors', a root of young potatoes, and a little joint of bacon all ready for me when I left for home. 'That,' Ethel said, 'is a treat for "himself",' the name she has conferred on my better half.

ANOTHER KIND OF MAGIC

I had spent a wonderful memorable day with my two old friends, one that I should remember for many years to come.

Pick all tail-end fruits—raspberries, strawberries, gooseberries, black and red currants—place in an earthenware crock and add a gallon of boiling water to every 4 lb of fruit.

Leave for four days stirring daily. Strain through a jelly bag. Add 3 lb sugar to every gallon of liquid. Heat very gently until sugar has dissolved (stirring all the time). Pour back into crock. Leave to ferment for another four days. Bottle off, corking lightly until all working has ceased.

Ethel's Raspberry Preserve

4 LB RASPBERRIES
5 LB GRANULATED SUGAR
½ OZ BUTTER (TO GREASE THE SAUCEPAN)

Put the raspberries onto a large meat dish and put into a warm oven. Place the sugar on another large dish and put that also in the oven. When they are hot tip both fruit and sugar into a large saucepan over a very low flame and continue to beat the fruit and sugar together until the sugar is completely dissolved. Pour into jars and tie down. This will keep for years.

8

'TEMPORY MOVE'

IT was early Autumn before Mark and his brother
moved 'up the top end cottage'. Missus-next-
door followed the week after, and these two neighbours, who for so many years had lived side by side
in the old cottages, were neighbours again in more
modern surroundings. At least they would be spend-
ing the winter there, for as I rode past the old
cottages I noticed that 'they builder chaps' hadn't
started work on them. Already every window pane
had been broken and Missus-next-door's roof looked
as if it would cave in at any moment.

Mark had got the sheep grazing nice and handy;
it is'nt often that they are penned so near his cottage
that he can pop off home at midday and get a fresh
cup of tea.

Mark was eager for me to see all over his 'tem-
pory home' as he called it; it certainly was an im-
provement on the old place. He chattered excitedly
as we walked round the comfortable little house.

'The best thing we done fer years was come up
yer to live,' he went on, 'when we comes home at
night thas just like a bakehouse oven in this livin'
room, arter that bin shut up all day. See this
"Aggur" cookin' thing, thas what keeps the house

warm, and thurs always plenty of 'ot water. And if I 'angs my old jackuts up affor we goes to bed they be nice and dry by mornin', and we can 'ave a bath just when we likes.

'When we come up yer fust go awf, Missus-next-door said that 'er 'ad a bath every day fer a week—didn't like to waste the water 'er said—strikes me 'er had more baths in that week than 'ers had in a twelvemonth down at t'other place. Course, when you 'ave 'ad to carry all yer water in and out fer so many years, you gets careful like, and all these luxuries what we got up yer took a bit of gettin' used to.

'Ah'n flush lavatories we got too, just outside the back door; none of that traipsin' up the garden no more. And what do you think of ower garden now then? Some difference to what that was when we fust come up yer.'

Mark must have worked like a Trojan to get the garden as ship-shape as it was. Only a few months ago it had looked like a wilderness. 'Course 'twas the wrong time of the year to plant much,' Mark said, as he proudly showed me a good bed of spring cabbage plants. 'Just got they in on time,' he went on, 'you should always get yer spring cabbage in by Michaelmas, then they got a good start affor the ground gets cold; an' I got me a few Gilly flowers and Sweet Williams planted too.'

What a wonderful gardener he was, I thought, to

have turned a wilderness into such a tidy plot. Still, I supposed it was something that he had inherited from his father.

'I can't understand fellows these days,' Mark said, as we wandered back down the long garden path, 'they be fer ever buyin' a bag of this and a bag of that to try and make the tackle in thur gardens grow; this is what they wants,' he went on, prodding his stick into a great pile of farmyard manure, 'you can't beat it, nobody never used anything else years ago.

'Ah-h, and when we was young we 'ad to go out with a bucket and shovel and collect hoss-muck; plenty about thur was, fer hosses was used fer most everything. Nowadays if you goes out to gather some 'arter they've 'ad one a they Jimmykana things, folks looks at you as if you be daft. A power-

ful lot of good hoss-muck does. Ah'h brings the
colour out in the roses that do.

I've told you before that my old father was a gardener, up at the big house, and 'e swore by animal
manure, and they growed some good crops in they
days.

'He used to tell we all sorts of tales of a winter's
night when we was all at home. Course I can't
remember 'um all. but thur's one or two as I shall
never forget.

'Thur was this man he knew whose daughter was
gettin' married—mind you the old fellow 'ad begun
to think as 'er was never goin' to get wed fer 'er
was goin' on fer fifty before any chap looked at 'er.
Anyhow this old fellow was goin' to give his daughter away, and the gel wantin' the weddin' to be all
posh-like said to 'er father—"Dad, you'll have to
get a new hat. I byent goin' to church with you
with that old 'un, you've had him this twenty years
as I knows on".

'So come Saturday the old fellow walks into the
nearest town, four miles away, to buy himself a new
trilby.

'He gets back 'ome about five hours later without
a new hat. "And why didn't you get a hat", the
daughter said, her was in a rare old temper 'cos the
weddin' was the next week and the old man
wouldn't be able to go shoppin' again before the
great day.

' "Well", the old chap replied, "they 'addent got one me size. I went into every shop and the biggest any of 'um 'ad was size 7⅜ and you knows that I takes a 15½ collar and my head's bigger than my neck 'ent it now."

'Darned old fool, wasn't he!' Mark said, and we laughed while he poured out another cup of tea and he went on story telling.

'And another tale that 'e used to tell we was about the village postman. You see my gel, it wasent only letters that they 'ad to deliver years ago, oh no, twas a recognised thing fer the postman to pick up the medicine from the Doctor's surgery and deliver it at the same time as he delivered the post, specially to people as lived in out-lying places. Course, in they days medicine 'ad to be paid for, and thur was an extra charge on the bottles, so it was very precious stuff specially to the working class.

'Well, one winter's morning Postman White was cycling off on his rounds, there'd been a frost over-night and the roads was like glass. Suddenly he skidded—he went one way and his bike the other and the contents of his bag scattered all over the road.

'The letters was all right, but a bottle of medicine that he was carrying for old Mrs. Ward was smashed. Now the postman noticed that on a piece of broken glass the label was still intact, so 'e put that carefully in his pocket. When 'e got to Mrs.

Ward's he told the old lady that her medicine wasent ready, but that he'd be sure and bring it the next day.

'When he got home that night, the first thing he done was to ask his wife if 'er'd got some Epsom salts in the house, lucky fer him 'er had. So 'e dissolved some in some hot water, and when twas cooled down a bit 'e fills up another medicine bottle with the mixture, then 'e steamed the label off that bit of broken glass and stuck it on the one containing the Epsoms and delivered it to Mrs. Ward the next morning without battin' an eyelid.

'About a couple of weeks arter 'e called on the old lady again, this time with a letter.

' "Ah'h Postman," she said, "I've been wanting to see you," and the first thing Postman White thought was that 'ed bin caught out. Then Mrs. Ward said, "Could you call at the Doctor's and ask him if he would please send I another bottle of medicine—the same sort as he sent last time. That have done I a power of good, I ent felt so well fer years."

'Mind you I dun't know how 'e got out of that 'un I'm sure, still I'll bet he had many a chuckle about they salts, I knows I have,' Mark said as he looked

at his watch. "Well, this won't do my wench, we've had a good chatter and now tis time to get back to the sheep, be you comin' to 'ave a look at um?"

'No, not today,' I told him, and as I turned my bike towards home Mark whistled for the dogs and went swinging down the lane.

9

'TATERING TALES'

THE beautiful autumn weather that we were having certainly suited the gang of potato pickers. Picking up spuds is hard work, but if the sun shines this irksome task is made much easier.

We'd had a few slight frosts, for this was mid-October. Already some of the leaves on the elms and oaks were golden, and dew-wet cobwebs hung like miniature cartwheels on every twig and bough. There were blackberries in the hedge—gleaming black and shiny—but we country people don't pick them after October the 10th because after that date they say 'the devil's piddled on them'. But I think the proper explanation is that by mid-October we've usually had a few frosts and this, along with the misty mornings, makes the fruit go mouldy and it would upset the stomach if eaten.

It is pleasant working out in the afternoon sun. A few of us have stripped off our warm jumpers. Some of the women have brought their young children with them and the youngsters play contentedly, building castles in the rich brown earth. The field that we are working in is bounded by water; I am fortunate enough to be working at the river edge, and in the quiet moments I've caught sight of some beautiful pink speckled trout, and the water rats swimming into their holes in the river bank. One of the tractor drivers pointed out a badger's sette to us, but of course there was no sign of Brock.

One day we caught a glimpse of a Kingfisher, but only for a fleeting moment did we see the flash of its brilliant blue wings. A few late scabious bloom on the verge-sides and in the hedge the sloes are almost ripe. As soon as we've finished spudding I shall be back to gather some for wine making.

It is rather sad that this season will see the end of the 'potato picking gangs' at least in this area. Because, one by one, the farmers are buying huge potato-picking machines which only need three or four men to operate. But this year, and for more years than some of the old 'uns want to remember, gangs of housewives have earned pin-money this way each autumn. So too have a few local retired men, who usually load up the trailers with full sacks of spuds or help to store them in the sheds and barns.

Only a few years back most of the farmers round here stored their potato crops in great long clamps outside in the fields, where they were covered first with straw and then with soil to keep out the frost. But the indoor method that they are using now is much easier and there is no risk of frost.

One man who has helped with the potato harvest for years is Jack Brookes, an upright seventy-five-year-old. He comes from one of the other villages and rides to work on his wife's bike—'Cyant cock me leg over me own these days,' he told me. 'I be that ett up with the rhumatics.'

For nearly fifty years he had been a gardener, but retired when he was sixty-five. Now, like us, he joins in with the potato harvest. 'Provides I with a bit of baccy money and keeps I out of the wife's way fer a bit,' he said laughingly one day.

Sometimes I help with the heavy lifting jobs, and work alongside Jack, and we chatter away as we carefully store the hundreds of tons of potatoes in the huge old stone barns.

'Ah, I started work when I was thirteen at that old mill in your village, fer a shilling a week,' he told me. 'I used to have to walk four miles over the fields to get thur. Three or four lads from our village worked thur too and we used to sing and laugh on our way to work, and we used to pinch turnips from Farmer Bank's fields too. I allus was fond of turnips, I reckons they does you a power of good, ah, and walkin' do too,' he went on, 'I shouldn't be as fit as I be today if I hadn't walked the hundreds of miles that I have.

'I was only earnin' four and six a week when I was seventeen, then one day our mother heard that Lord Parks wanted a garden boy—they kept eight gardeners and six garden boys—and they was good people to work for too. So I smartens meself up and went along to see if I could get the job, but there was twelve other young boy-chaps there after it. And I thought how disappointed our mother would be if I didn't get it. "Be polite and honest" she said to me before I left home that mornin'. Well, I got the job and I stopped there till I retired, ah, and I was head gardener for the last fifteen years.'

He has been married twice and refers to the ladies in his life as 'my wife as is', and 'my wife as was' when he's talking about them. We were chatting about cooking one day and he said, 'Thur was one fer cookin' my wife as was, 'er could make a meal fer seven of us out of nothin' but a few bones and vegetables out of me garden—and the gret big currant duffs 'er used to make, full of lumps of suet they was, "butchers plums" we used to call they pieces of suet. My wife as is, 'ers a good cook, but her'll never come up to my wife as was, not fer cookin' 'er won't, 'ers all fer this new-fangled way of doing it, a packet of this and a tin of that and thurs yer dinner; wholesome enough I suppose, but I sometimes wishes as how I could set down to one a they smashing dinners my wife as was used to turn out.

'Still, its no good thinking about that now is it?' he went on, 'thur 'ent many people as makes suet puddin's these days, spoils thur figgers they reckons, ah, and I should think all this liftin' 'ull do your figger a bit of good won't it?' he said to me as we emptied the sacks of potatoes piled high on the waiting trailers. The tractor drivers were certainly coming into the barn with their huge loads at a rare pace, the weather had been good for days and the ground was dry and firm, and everyone was in a good mood. Each day we were all allowed to take a few spuds home. I usually picked out some big ones, 'jackty Taters' as we call them, for field potatoes always seem so much bigger than those we grow ourselves. The crop this farmer grows are *Majestic*, which suit the soil very well in these parts. Later on some of us will be asked to come and help sort this crop, but that won't be until January or February. At last the cry goes up 'dinner time' and Jack and I carry a bale of straw outside and sit in the sun to have our meal. We are certainly ready for the break, for we've been hard at it since nine o'clock.

'I never did tell you about old Charlie Douser did I?' Jack said after we'd finished eating. 'He lived in the same village as I did when I was a youngster. Do you know I never heard him called anything else but Charlie *Douser*, but he must have had another name. Like as not he was the first fireman that we ever had in our village, and you never saw him without a long pole, with a piece of flannel nailed on the end in one hand, and an old bucket with water in, in the other.

'You see most of the cottages and some of the barns was straw-thatched, and a spark from a bon-

fire or one from the blacksmith's forge could have
easily set the village on fire, if it hadn't been for old
Charlie and his bit of flannel on the end of his pole.
Course, the only water we had was in the wells—
there was a lot about the village, at the backs of
the cottages. And although Douser always carried
water with him, he could soon get more if a fire got
out of hand—not that one ever did, but there was
one or two near goes as I remember.

'When a fire did break out, the warnin' was given
just by a good loud "holler" of "fire! fire!". All the
houses was clustered close together and within minutes old Douser would come runnin' up the street,
his long legs coverin' the ground at a rare old pace.
He was one of the tallest men I've ever seen, about
six foot eight he was, with gret long arms, so with
these and his pole he could easily reach the roof of
any of the low thatched cottages. He'd work like a
trojan and have that fire out in no time at all.

'Of course winter was Douser's busiest time, with
all the cottage fires lit for cooking, and firework
time kept him busy too. Though thur wasent much
money for fireworks in them days, but we used to
have a bonfire and gather sacks of conkers and
chuck 'em on thur, and they'd bang and explode
better than any fireworks.

'But thur's one bonfire night as I shall never
ferget. We boys was havin' a merry old time, goin'
round the village from one kid's bonfire to another,

when suddenly there was an urgent shout to "get the kids out of the way! quick, get 'em off the road!" And we was shoved into a walled garden. We peered over the top and saw this flamin' torch like a gret ball of fire tearin' down the hill towards the centre of the village. The women shrieked, kids cried, dogs barked, and old mother Broadbent flung 'er apron over 'er head and shouted that the end of the world was drawin' near. But old Douser had done some quick thinkin', he guessed what the fire ball was, he'd seen the lads of the village go swaggerin' off up the hill laughin' and chatterin', thur eyes full of mischief. Douser noticed too that workmen had been mendin' the top road and they'd left barrels of tar by the roadside. The boys had set one of these tar barrels alight and had started it on its journey down the hill. From the garden wall we watched absolutely terrified as that flamin' barrel got nearer and nearer. "Quick, give us a hand!" Douser shouted and he lifted farmer Dore's big iron gate from its hinges. Six or seven men rushed to help him and as the barrel reached the houses they held the great big gate right in the pathway of the fast movin' barrel, to divert it away from the cottages at the bottom of the hill. It was travellin' at such a rate that it nearly knocked that strong body of men off thur feet. Then it smashed against the opposite wall—paused—then went careerin' down the road past the church and into the village

pond. Them boys come down the hill a bit shame-
faced I can tell you, they didn't realise what a lot of
damage they could have done. Anyhow the boys'
fathers dealt with them, awf come thur leather belts
and every lad had the biggest thrashin' of thur
lives, in front of the whole village too.

'Mind you,' old Jack went on, 'nobody ever done
anything like that ever again; which was just as well
really, because the next year a "widder" woman
from the Midlands come to our village fer a holiday
and, do you know, 'er swept old Douser off his feet,
married him and took him off to spend the rest of
his life in a crowded city. But we often used to talk
about him and the day he saved our village.'

A tractor roared into the yard, the women rose
stiffly from where they'd rested their weary bones
and walked slowly down the potato rows, ready to
start again. Old Jack and I reluctantly got to our
feet, ready to start another three hours hard work.
I should have to wait 'till the next dinnertime before I heard more stories from him.

'Talkin' about blacksmiths,' he said to me a few
days later, 'did you know old Gossop Taylor, he
only retired last year? He was a darned good smithy
too, I used to walk down to see him most mornin's.
Nobody took his job on when he give up; pity, thas
a nice little place. Course, three or four of we
retired men used to go in thur fer a chatter every
day, that was nice and warm in thur too, but talk

about a dark little hole, couldn't see to tell the truth
I used to say. I did laugh one mornin',' he went on,
'it happened to be one a they very dull winter days
and old Perce Hill walks in and he said to Gossop
"I can't understand you workin' in the dark like
this, why dun't you 'ave a skylight fixed in this yer
roof?"

' "Ah well" Gossop said, "If I done that, the kids
'ud chuck stwons up an' break the glass, wouldn't
'um?"

' "Well" old Perce said, "You could allus throw
a sack over it so as they couldn't see it, couldn't
you?"

'Folks do say some comical things sometimes
don't 'um my gel', he went on, 'we had a fellow
livin' next door to we durin' the war, 'e come from
up north somewhere and damn me if I could understand him fer ages. He hadn't bin livin' next to we
very long when he knocks at our door. I goes and he
ses in a foreign sort of language, "can I have a loan
of yer tomboy?"

' "Me what?" I ses.

' "Yer tomboy," he ses.

'Well I looked at him and he looked at I, neither
of us knew what to say—for I didn't know what he
wanted—he knew but couldn't tell me, well not in
my way of talkin' anyway.

'So I ses to him, "I got no tomboy here, all our
gels be married and lives away." Then he burst out

124

laughin' and said, "I don't want to borrow your
daughter, I wants to mend the missus's shoes and I
wants to borrow your tomboy to do it with." I still
didn't cotton on as to what he meant so I ses to him,
"you come and have a look in the shed, perhaps you
can show me what 'tis you wants", and do you
know what he was on about my gel, he wanted to
borrow me iron foot. Course we had a darn good
laugh after that.

'Ah, and another funny little bit I heard the other
day made I laugh, though really it was quite a
serious thing. I happened to overhear the village
grave digger tellin' a stranger about his work, and
this was just the words he used: "Ah, I be grave
digger in this yer village an' I takes a pride in me
work. I digs 'um good and deep, then when they've
laid the coffin in, I don't just chuck the earth
straight in, oh no, I packs moss and pebbles round
and makes it good and firm, ah, and when I've
finished with 'um they be thur fer life."

'You see my gel, our little cottage is just agen
the churchyard and thats how I overheard him a
talkin'. And before I fergets, my wife as is said to be
sure and ask you to come and have a cup of tea with
us, as soon as the spuddin's over.'

But the spuddin' hung on longer than we thought.
We had a few wet days that held us up and then
when we did start again the going was pretty hard,
with tractors and loads of potatoes getting stuck in

the mud. The gang of women got smaller too, for the ones with the little children stayed at home. A muddy wet cold tater field is no place for a small child. And what had started out as a nice open-air job in the sun ended with mud up to our eyebrows and we were all thankful when the last load was carefully stored away.

However, a few days later we had some more nice warm days, 'St. Luke's little summer' we call those last few bright days of Autumn. So I went along to gather some sloes that I had seen growing in the hedge of one of the potato fields. I make both Sloe Wine and Sloe Gin—the gin being much more expensive and much more potent than the wine; both are very nice. The trouble is we only seem to get one good year in about four with sloes, so I make an extra amount when they are plentiful to make up for the poor seasons.

After I'd gathered as many as I thought I needed, and prickled myself on the sharp thorns, I made my way to the village where Old Jack and 'my wife as is' lived. They were so pleased to see me, and I was shown round the tidy garden before going indoors for a cup of tea.

'Come and have a look at the rest of the cottage' Jack's wife said, 'though tis very small, just two up and two down, still 'tis big enough for we—tin bath, and lavatory down the bottom of the garden —we've never been used to anything else so it

don't come amiss to us,' she told me happily. Old Jack followed behind close at our heels. 'I wants you to see the lovely view we got from the bedroom window,' he said. The cottage overlooked the churchyard.

'See,' he went on, 'the ground drops down sharp just beyond the church and then it rises again, see that wood, thas about four miles away, "Pinnocks" we calls it, thurs nothing nicer than to lay a-bed on a summer mornin' just when thats gettin' light and watch the daylight float over the wood and the fields, and the birdsong regler wakes you up but we don't mind. I brought the vicar up yer when he first took over this parish, and he was lookin' out of the window and he said "what a wonderful panorama Mr. Brookes, you are lucky to live in such a delightful spot." So I ses "Yes sir I am, and

do you know that you and I can see beyond the grave." He turns round and gives me such a funny look and said seriously "I have no claim for that, if you have". Then I grinned and said, "just take a look at your churchyard sir, and the graves, and the fields beyond—that's what I meant, we can see beyond the graves." Course he had a chuckle about it after, he's got used to I and my little jokes now.

'I thinks we be in for a hard winter,' Jack said as we settled ourselves down for more tea. 'I was sayin' to my wife the other day, the onions have got a good thick skin on um, thas a sure sign of a cold winter.'

'Haven't you heard that little rhyme about onions?' she asked me:

> *Onion skin very thin,*
> *Mild Winter coming in;*
> *Onion skin thick and tough*
> *Coming winter cold and rough.*

'And the moles,' Jack cut in, 'they be going down already, thas another sure sign. You see they goes down deep cos the worms and insects what they lives on goes down, and the reason for that is so that they will be frost free. I wonder what warns 'um that ther's a hard winter a-head.'

'Ah,' he went on, changing the subject, 'I'll tell you about the time I made ten shillings in about two minutes, easiest money I ever earned in me life. Twas like this, I was walkin' home from me allotment one day and Squire Mayson comes up to I.

' "Oh Brooks, you are just the man I want to see" he said, "I wonder if you would come and have a look at my orchard, its been laid down with new fruit trees this two years and there's no sign of growth yet". Course I knew what 'e was on about, I'd noticed they trees meself and I knew they wasent doing very well, and I knew the reason. Mind you I didn't let on to him as I'd noticed 'um.

'Well we reaches the orchard gate and the squire goes to open it. Beggin' your pardon sir, thurs no need to go in, I ses, I can see whats wrong with 'um from here. You see, you had the orchard carefully ridged and furrowed, thats all right, the mistakes in the plantin'. Your men set the tree roots in the furrows, tis too damp, how would you like your feet in water all the time sir? All you wants to do is to get the trees replanted on the ridges, they roots will go down if they wants a drink. Then the squire puts his hand in his pocket and gives me a ten shilling note, that seemed like a fortune because at that time I wasent earning no more than three pounds a week.

'Mind you, a gardener has to be a very knowledgeable man and a tidy man too. You see, me gel, a gardener's like a housemaid, 'e makes the beds and emps the pots, no offence mind you, but you must admit tis right.

'We shall get quite a sharp frost tonight I reckon,' he said as he saw me to the gate, 'see how clear and red that sun's going down, good job you got your sloes today, they can stand a few mild frosts, but if that's a bit sharp they goes all soft like and no good at all.'

'Don't wait till next taterin' season before you comes again,' his wife said, ''e do so love somebody to chatter to.'

I didn't remind her that we had, in fact, just witnessed the end of potato picking by hand, the end of a way of life that had lasted since potatoes were first grown in this country many years ago. The machines would be a much easier way of harvesting them, and more economical; but not half as much fun, and I for one was going to miss it.

Mark's Sloe Gin

1 LB SLOES
3 OZ CASTOR SUGAR
1½ PINTS GIN

Wipe the sloes clean and prick each one several times with a large needle, throw into a Kilner type jar, now add the sugar and screw down the lid. Leave until all the sugar has dissolved. Now add the gin and remember to shake the jar slightly about every other day for three months. Strain and bottle, cork tightly and store for a year (if possible).

10

SHIP DAGS

THE cold hard weather of the past winter had given way to a lovely early spring. Already the snow-white blackthorn blossoms showed up like patches of mist against the still bare branches in the hedgerows.

The birds were taking advantage of the mild days, blackbirds especially were chack chacking away, announcing to the world that they had staked a claim in the nearby hedge. All around the fields

had been planted with corn, carefully harrowed, then left clean, tidy and bare to await the sun and rain of April. In the giant elm trees which skirted the hamlet where Mark lived, dozens of squawking jet black rooks were busily tidying up their last year's nest.

Mark was in the garden. He already had a visitor, a smartly dressed pale-faced young man; they were gazing into a trench which the shepherd had dug, a long deep trench which reached from where they were standing to the wall.

'You waants tu dig one like this fer yer kidney beans,' he was telling the young man, 'I allus do, I leaves it open like this for weeks to let the sun and air get into it before I fills it up with me dags, the finest thing in the world fer kidney beans is ship dags.'

The young man looked puzzled, 'What the devil are you talking about' he said laughingly to Mark.

'Well, you knaws what ship dags be surely, 'tis all that claggum tackle what we cuts awf 'um', Mark went on. 'You see about a month before the ship be sheared they 'as tu be tidied up, cos you can't send mucky fleeces away, an' when they ship eats too much young grass, arter being fed on swedes an' hay all winter, they gets what we calls the gripes an' instead of the muck leavin' 'um it gets all matted round the wool. Ent you ever sin a ship runnin' about with gret lumps of wool an'

muck round its backside? Well, this all 'as tu be
cut awf, then when shearin' time comes round they
be all nice and clean. What you waants tu do is to
get 'old of some a this an' fill yer kidney bean
trench up with it. You see, my boy, the wool 'elps
tu 'old the moisture an' the muck 'elps tu feed the
beans, an' if you does just what I tells yu, you'll 'ave
kidney beans as long as yer arm. I'll tell you what'
Mark said, 'if you likes tu come along sometime
early in May, I'll give you a sack of daggin's, I
shall be starting to clean the ship up then -ah-h,
about the fust week in May.'

'And talkin' about ship daggin', one spring I was
a doin' me daggin', I'd got some of the ship penned
up, sortin' out the ones with the dirty backsides
then cuttin' awf all the muck with a pair of hand
shears. I noticed that a car 'ad pulled up, and two
men and two women—thur wives I suppose, was
'aving a look round the countryside. Then the men
gets out of the car an' walks over tu see what I be
doin', and fer a few minutes watches I workin'
away. Then the ladies joined 'um. I'd just got 'old
of a ship what was fair clapered up with muck
round 'is backside an' one a these women takes one
look at what I be doin' an' said, "How disgusting"
tossin' her head in the air as 'er spoke.

'I looks up at 'er an' ses "What do you mean
disgusting Maam, if your Mother 'adnt done the
same thing fer you, you'd a bin in a fine pickle by

now I'll bet." Her just stood thur for a minute lookin' at I with 'er mouth open, then they all cleared off.

'I often wonders if I shall ever run against her again', Mark said, as we laughed over his tale.

'He's one a they town fellas' Mark told me, inclining his head towards the departing figure of the young man as he walked off down the lane, 'come to settle in these parts and don't know the next thing about gardenin', so I be goin' to give him some of my valuable advice fer what its worth.

'And talking about kidney beans, don't you ferget my wench, get 'um planted by Stow fair day May 12ths, we allus keeps to that date round these parts.'

'My next door neighbour said a funny thing to I the other day,' Mark went on, as we strolled up the garden path, ''e was tellin' I about a mole what had bin makin' a mess of his gardenin'. He said, "that old mole went zig-zag right across my seed bed— ah-h like a shot out of a gun 'e went." Damned old fool, how could summut go zigzag *and* like a shot out of a gun!

'I brought you a couple of mangolds home,' he went on, 'we opened the bury yesterday, just to give the cattle a bit of a change of grub, so I collared two of the biggest I could see, I knowed as you likes to make a drop of mangold wine about this time of the year.'

The mangolds lay on the path, they glowed bright orange and yellow in the pale afternoon sun.

'What's the news about your cottage? I've come over specially to find out when you're going back,' I asked him.

'Well the truth is my wench, we bent goin' back, we'd rather stay wur we be, you never see such a difference they've made to our old place—not the sort of home fer workin' chaps like we.'

'Whatever has happened? I thought you were longing to get back, and you've kept the garden planted too,' I cried.

'Well fust go awf they've put we a potty little front-room grate in—thas no good to we. I likes a fireplace wur you can set a pot with a bit of bacon on to boil—you got summut to watch then. Now if we went back thur, and we'd got a bit of bacon cookin' on the 'lectric stove, I should have to keep goin' in and out, from wur I was settin' by the fire, out to the kitchen to see if twas done—an' look at all the 'lectric I should use. And another thing, 'ow be I goin' to get my jackuts dry—sometimes I got six or more all soakin' wet arter that bin peltin' down with rain all day. And they've put the lavartory upstairs—now do you call that good plannin' for a couple of farm workers to live in—an' we a-comin' 'ome from work all clapered up with mud? No, I told Gaffer as it 'ouldn't suit we at all, and if its all the same to 'im we'll stop wur we be.'

'What about Missus-next-door? Is she going to stay too?'

'No, thas the funny part, 'er likes 'um 'er ses, and 'ers goin' back as soon as 'ers is finished, but we shall stay wur we be.'

I could see that nothing that I or anyone said would budge Mark and his brother from the warm comfortable cottage, so I just let him ramble on.

'Ah-h we got a very good system ower Fred and me, we does most of our work on a Sunday, 'e farms out the house while I does the cookin'—I recons to make a couple of big fruit cakes and a pie affor I puts the Sunday joint in. Then once a week me sister comes and does the bedrooms out and does the washin'—thas 'ow we manages.

'But thas enough about our troubles,' Mark said, 'I bin a-thinkin' of one er two tales to tell you, I promised I'd try and think of some my old Dad told I. I never did tell you the one about Silas Moore did I? He was the village carter round these parts, journeying between Oxford and all the villages that lay along the way, and he'd fetch and carry most anythin' folk wanted. Used to go shoppin' fer the ladies too, 'eed buy combs and corsets, flannelette nightgowns and calico knickers, he didn't mind what it was, 'e took it all in his stride.

'But 'e 'ad one fault, he used to get dead drunk. Regular on a Wednesday when 'e come home from Oxford Market he'd call at all the pubs along the way, and affor 'e got home 'e was as tight as a tic.

'But 'e knowed when 'ed had enough and every Wednesday arternoon he'd pull up at a quiet spot called Bell Bridge and sleep it off.

'Well, one day some of the local farm labourers who was workin' in a nearby field thought they'd play a trick on the old carrier, and as soon as he dropped off to sleep they un-hitched his horses and turned 'um out into a field. Then one of the men sat under the cart and waited for old Silas to wake up.

'About five o'clock that arternoon Silas woke. He set bolt upright in the cart, then looked round fuddled-like, a-scratchin' 'is head, wonderin' where 'e was. Then 'e said to 'isself "Silas Moore, I recons you be dead, well if its I, that is, but if it ent I, who be I?"

'Then 'e noticed that his horses was gone and said "Well, if it is I, I've lost two hosses, but if it ent I, I've found a cart!"

'Mind you, my old Dad said that arter that episode Silas went a bit steady on the beer fer a while—but it didn't last long, he was soon sleepin' it awf again on Wednesday afternoons.

'Ah-h another tale I remembers was one 'e used to tell about the days when the corn was all cut with scythes and thur 'ud be six or seven men at a time scything away in a field at harvest time, and in they days twas right and proper fer the farmer who employed 'um to supply a certain amount of beer or cider for the men. And every now and then the gang of hot thirsty workers 'ould stop and each 'ould take a swig from the big stone jar—you knows the sort, with a handle near the narrow neck. The fellows 'ad a knack of restin' the jar on thur shoulder and the beer or cider was drunk straight out of it.

'Course the jar was always kept in the hedge to keep the drink cool-like.

'Well, a pal of my old dad's was called Sid Parker, and 'e used to work in one of these yer gangs and 'e told 'im about the way they cured one of the chaps who was a bit greedy like. Jimmy 'is name was, they reconed that 'e 'ad twice as much drink as 'tothers. So they played a trick on 'im. One day when they was workin' in the field old Sid come across a nest of new-born mice and he and the other fellows dropped um into the beer jar, they knew twas prit-near empty. When they got round to wur the jar was kept, Jimmy made a bee-line for it—allus first 'e was.

'He took a good long swig and finished the lot—then 'e coughed a bit and wiped 'is mouth with the back of 'is 'and and said, "that beer's got a bit thick. I recon farmer's got to the bottom of the barrel; that last drop had hops in, I know."

'Course the rest of the gang busted our laughin' and holdin' thur sides and the tears a-runnin' down thur cheeks.

'Then they told Jimmy what they'd done and 'e was as sick as a dog. But that larned 'im, 'e never reconed to take first swig of the jar after that.'

While Mark had been story-telling the sun had moved round to the West and had begun to set red and rosy, lighting up the fluffy clouds till they looked like candy floss.

'Ah-h, looks like another fine day tomorrow my gel, "red sky at night—shepherds' delight." Course you know what they ses when tis red sky in the mornin' don't you, red sky in the mornin'—shepherds' warnin', ploughboy take yer coat.'

I had to admit that I hadn't heard the last little bit about the coat, but then I was always learning new things from Mark. He was such a knowledge-able man—this man of the hills—he knew about the habits of birds and beasts, wind and weather, a man who during his long life had never been away for a holiday—never been away from the wide hills that he loved so much. Yet he was content—content and happy—a man that anyone would be glad to call his friend.

Jessie Pratley's Mangold Wine

½ OZ YEAST

5 LB MANGOLDS   2 LEMONS

1 GALLON WATER   2 ORANGES

3 LB SUGAR (EITHER DEMERARA OR LUMP
DEM MAKES A DARKER WINE)

Scrub the mangolds but do not peel. Cut into smallish pieces and place in a saucepan with the water. Boil until tender. Strain, add sugar and rinds of oranges and lemons to the strained liquid and boil for a further twenty minutes. Allow to cool. Add juice of lemons and oranges. Mix the yeast with a little castor sugar and place on top of the liquid. Leave to work for seven days. Strain and bottle lightly. (During the seven days while the wine is working keep the pan covered with a clean dry cloth.)

11

BILL BROWN AND HIS MISSUS

ONE thing about doing casual work for more than one farmer, is that you do meet a variety of people. And on one of the farms I made the acquaintance of Bill Brown. We had a lot in common, a genuine love of the soil and simple things of the countryside. So I always jumped at the chance to work alongside him for a few days. We found plenty to chatter about as we slashed away at weeds or singled out sugar beet.

This particular year Bill and I had been asked to help with the hoeing on the farm where at one time Bill had been fully employed, and although there was no need for him to work he loved to be asked. He would shake his old head and say to me, 'Ah, they can't do wi'out we old uns, we has to come and give 'um a hand every now and then.' Whether Old Bill included me when he said 'we old uns', I don't know. Bill, by the way, was in his seventies and I in my forties.

On this lovely May day we had been hoeing all morning, the sun hot on our backs as we worked. But despite the heat old Bill still wore his 'weskit', and thick cord trousers yorked up just below the knee, a striped working shirt, a large straw hat and heavy boots.

'I'll bet I be cooler than you', he said, eyeing my red sweating face and bare arms; he was too, yet I was clad in the minimum of clothes.

At dinnertime we sat in the cool of a giant elm tree, to have our 'vittalls'. Bill never called food anything else but 'vittalls'. It was either 'me mornin' vittalls, me nuncheon vittalls or me night vittalls'.

Some days we would sit and eat in complete silence, depending on how Bill felt. Other days he would tell me vivid stories of his youth; they might have been harder, but he reckoned that they were much happier times than the present ones. He used to say 'I be glad I was born in a cottage wur thur was allus piles of stew and mountains of dumplings'.

A young fellow who worked on the same farm went careering down the road on a great smelly tractor; this set old Bill going. 'Look at that damned young fool', he said, 'break his neck if 'e 'ent careful. The trouble is these days, if it 'ent got a seat on it, they don't want it. These young uns don't know nothin' about walking; our old gaffer always liked us to walk with our hosses— nowadays thas all they wants to do, set on they soulless things. But give I hosses anytime, they be near human, you can talk to 'um and they knows what you ses to 'um, too, and they got souls all right—that I be sure of. Course when I got retired from this estate me poor hosses got retired too; broke my heart to see they go off to the knackers yard, thur was years of good work in they hosses, same as thur was in I, and I be good fer another ten years and I be gone seventy. Course, when the old squire retired, and his son took over—'e as we be working for now—twas very different. "Clear out all the old stuff" he said, I heard him, "men and machinery, and the horses will have to go", 'e said—a liability tha's what 'e called us old uns. Fair knocked I over fust go off, but they was very good to we really.

'Ah, the young master come to I just before I retired and said, "You and your wife can stay in your cottage as long as you like, you shall have it in writing." And he said they would give I a small pension, so they couldn't be fairer than that.

'Course I've worked yer all me life, boy and man —come to help in the stables when I was twelve and stayed yer regler till I was sixty-five.

'Mind you, this young gaffer got the right ideas —got to move with the times, but with all thur new-fangled methods, they won't produce no better crops 'er cattle than we did. His father was always winnin' prizes at cattle shows, and 'e'd let his men go in fer ploughin' and thatchin' contests, and I'll bet you nine times out of ten twas ower chaps what won.'

We had a slight pause while old Bill finished off his bread and cheese. Then he went on. 'Lot of

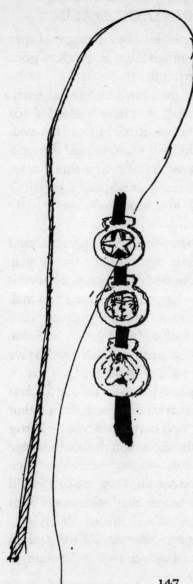

alterations goin' on up at the big house. Young master 'ent goin' to live thur—well so 'um ses. I've heard tell that they've sold it for an agricultural research place, he's goin' to have the bailiff's house done up fer 'e and his young wife; plenty big enough fer them 'e ses.

'Then all they outbuildings and stables be goin' to be made into up-to-date flats and houses fer the farm workers and thur wives, thas why they didn't want the cottages as we old uns lives in.

'Mind you, I shouldn't want to move, not at my

time of life; we've lived in ower cottage all 'er married life, and my missus 'ave lived thur since her was about seven or eight.

'When I retired they let I have all me old horse brasses. Carter 'e ses to I, you have these, I don't see as how anybody else is entitled to them but you. So we've got 'um all hung up, and me old drover's whip. The missus keeps they brasses shone up a treat. I should like as many pounds as times I've polished 'um, when I was working—lovely they brasses allus looked.

'Twas a nice sound they made too, a-jinglin' and janglin', and them hosses that proud, a-tossin' thur 'eads up when folks admired 'um—ah-h hosses be near human, I tell 'e what, the last two I had was called Beauty and Rastus, and I recons as they knowed every word I said to 'um.'

Here we had another pause in this fascinating tale of Bill's, while he swilled down his food with a bottle of cold tea. 'Nothin' like cold tea for a thirst quencher,' Bill was always telling me, 'and never drink between meals, 'specially when you're doing field work. Tis fatal, the more you drinks the more you wants to.'

'Funny thing', Bill went on, 'My missus ses to I the other day, "you might think this queer" 'er said, but I been thinkin' of old Beauty and Rastus such a lot today—keeps wondering if they goes to heaven along a we". So I ses to 'er, "whatever

made you think about them, they bin dead this past
ten or eleven years, you gets such daft idea's in
that old 'ead of yours."

' "Never mind," 'er said, "I just can't get 'um
out of me mind, keeps wondering if tha's what they
green pastures be for, what they sings about."
Fancy my old missus a-talkin' like that. I told her
the older 'er gets the sillier 'er gets.'

But I could see that what Bill's missus had said
had moved the old fellow and he turned his head
away and blew his nose very hard.

Time to go back to the hoeing—the sun beat
down, and the sultry afternoon wore on.

'Get some thunder affor long I shouldn't wonder,'
Bill said, when we stopped for a breather at the end
of one of the rows, 'thur's a lot of they wapsy flies
about, proper spitful they be too.'

We were both very thankful when five o'clock
came. Bill looked tired and suddenly very old. He
ought to give up this casual work, but I suppose
he'd worked hard all his life and to use his own
expression, 'he just couldn't abide to set still'.

The next day Bill didn't turn up for work, and as
I moved steadily up and down the endless rows I
couldn't help feeling just a bit worried. The farm
foreman had been to say that Bill had had a bad
turn in the night and wouldn't be at work today,
but he added, 'if I know anything of old Bill he'll
turn up tomorrow, you see.'

But old Bill didn't turn up again—he died the following day.

I called to see Mrs. Bill a little while after; I'd heard that she was giving up her cottage and going to live with her youngest sister in a nearby village. 'I can't stay here be meself,' she told me, ''tis no good, I be for ever seeing my old Bill everywhere. Its best fer I to go and live with our Dolly, 'ers a widdow woman too. We always did get on well together, and I don't see why we still can't,' and she busied about, carefully wrapping her crockery in newspaper.

We began to talk about Bill, for he and I had worked together so often, and I knew just when 'my missus made her jams and wines' and when old Bill put his early 'taters in.

I told her that Bill had mentioned about the horses Beauty and Rastus and of her thinking of them so. 'Ah-h that was a most peculiar thing,' she went on, 'do you know, I'd had them horses on my mind for days. Then that night as he died, all he wanted was they horse brasses, and 'e kept asking for 'um, so I gets up on a chair and fetched 'um down off the wall. Then he said to I, "we shall want these soon missus" and he stroked 'um and went off to sleep. I tried to take them away from him—thought that he'd lie on them and make himself uncomfortable like, but he'd got hold of them that tight. So I left them there.

'Then about four o'clock—just as twas getting
light and the birds was a-singing thur little hearts
out—he wakes up, and seemed bright and well, he
did. So I ses to him, what about a nice cup of tea
Bill? He looked up at me and said, "I got no time
to set yer drinkin' tea missus, I be awf to fetch
Beauty and Rastus, and we be a-goin' out into the
fields agen, out into the green pastures". And that
was it, he just smiled and died, still caught hold of
his brasses he was too.'

A few days later I saw a tractor and trailer carrying Bill's Missus's bit of furnture over to her
sister's, and a pathetic little lot it was too. Mrs.
Bill had told me that she was going on ahead. 'I
don't want to see the old stuff going out of the
cottage,' she said, 'I wants to remember the place
when twas full of life, not empty and quiet.'

About a twelvemonth after old Bill died, I was
back on the same farm again. The first thing I did
was to ask if anyone was living in Bill's old cottage.
One of the young tractor drivers answered and said:
'A couple of months arter Mrs. Bill left, the gaffer
had it pulled down—twas falling down anyroad—
no good for nothing. We used the stones and rubble
to fill up the ruts in the gateways.'

That evening something compelled me to go to
the spot where the cottage had been. A stranger
would have never known that there had ever been
anything there, other than a field. For now, where

the old place had been, corn was just coming through—the little cottage had stood in the corner of the field, and now it was just a field, with a lighter patch of earth that the mortar and stone dust had left. This was the only visible sign that anything had ever been there.

I walked about the patch of light soil—little bits of broken crockery that Bill's missus had used had been brought to the surface with the ploughing. I felt sad and quite depressed that this happy little home was no more—Bill had gone and his Missus I heard was ill.

The sun was low in the sky as I turned to go home. Suddenly I saw something glinting on the top soil; I picked it up, and knew at once what it was. It seemed as if old Bill was by my side telling me: 'When we got married I was only earning sixteen bob a week, and my old dad said to me, "I got nothin' else to give you but this—always keep it and you'll never be hard up". Twas a golden sovereign. So I had it put on me watch chain; twas safe thur, fer I should have had to have it cut off to have spent it. Anyhow it always looked nice, and as me old Dad said, while I'd got that I couldn't be hard up—mind you, thur was hundreds of times that we could have done with that to spend, but somehow we always managed.

'But a few years ago I lost it while I was a-digging me garden; we searched every bit of soil

over but we never found it. You see it had bin on
that chain so long, it had worn right through. In
time we give up looking for it, give it up as a bad
job, but I should have liked my eldest to have had
it.' Poor old Bill, I thought, never mind, I'll ride
over to the village and give it to his Missus; it
might cheer her up a bit.

About three days after my find I cycled over to
see Missus Bill—it was about six miles to the
village where she lived. It was a lovely fresh spring
day, and the air was like champagne. Everywhere
was the lush green growth of a Cotswold spring-
time. Cattle, sheep and lambs were enjoying the
fresh young grass, larks sang high above in the
warm sunshine. It was one of those rare, May days
that you never forget.

When I reached the edge of the village I began
to look out for someone to ask where Mrs. Bill
lived. I knew the house was called Kingfisher
Cottage, but had no idea where it was.

A woman busy gardening told me the way. 'Ah'
she said, 'you means her what come over from
Tansworth to live with her sister, their cottage is
about the tenth from here. But', she added, 'you're
a bit late arn't you?'

I thanked her and moved off quickly, wondering whatever she meant. As I neared Kingfisher
Cottage I could see a little knot of people by the
gate; they were mostly middle-aged and elderly,

BILL BROWN AND HIS MISSUS

and dressed in black. They stood quiet and still while men lifted a coffin on to a hearse. I knew at once why the woman had said 'you are a bit late arn't you?'

155

12

COTSWOLD SPRING

IT was nearing the end of May. I had heard from Mark that he had started to shear the sheep.

'We are in the old barn at Little Brackton', he wrote. Little Brackton is a very small village, one tiny church built in 1612, a manor house, five or six farmworkers' cottages and some old cotswold barns.

Mark had told me once that Little Brackton had been 'a smartish place' centuries ago. This could easily have been so, for there were several over-grown old orchards and many hillocks and mounds as if quite a number of buildings had once been dotted about. Now the manor house was the home of the farm foreman and the little church was only used occasionally.

Yet it was situated in a delightful valley, sheltered on three sides by wide high hills—green and lush, lush and green, that's how it looked on this lovely May day. Many of the fields in this quiet spot were carpeted with green and gold—gold from the millions of buttercups and dandelions which spattered the green grass. Giant Whitsuntide candles (horse chestnut blossom) graced the old knarled trees, and hedges of creamy-white May garlanded some of the fields.

COTSWOLD SPRING

'All in a rush with richness', is what Gerard Manley Hopkins wrote of the month of May, and how right he was.

In the little copsies and woods, carpets of blue-bells glowed almost purple in the trees' shade. On

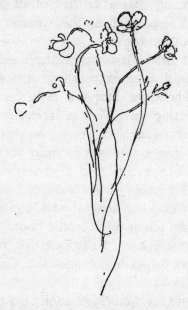

the verge-sides sweet-smelling cowslips nodded their key-like bunches of flowers. When I was a youngster we children used to sometimes call them 'Freckled Faces' because of the orange markings on the flowers, another country name for them is 'fairy flower'. A few late primroses, 'pimiroses' my gramp used to call them, bloomed on the bank. And the air was scented with the delicate perfume from the pink and white crab-apple blossom.

I crossed the field toward the barn where the shearing was in progress. Dotted about were dozens of sheep already white and shorn. It must be wonderful for the animals to be free of all their thick winter wool, especially as the weather was uncommonly hot for May.

The great tithe barn where Mark and another man were hard at work was over three hundred years old. The huge door was open on one side, and the sweating men were in their shirt-sleeves. It was fascinating to watch them, how gently they handled the sheep and how skilfully they sheared them. Now-a-days they use electrically operated shears, but for many years Mark had sheared by hand. A third man was kept busy folding and rolling the fleeces and piling them on the floor.

When Mark saw me he stopped for 'blowings', a few minutes to get his breath back. Carefully he rolled a cigarette.

'Look at um my wench', he said, holding out his enormous hands to me. 'Soft as a baby's bum they be. 'Tis the lanolin what does that', he went on. 'Thas wur yer lanolin comes from my gel, out of ship's wool. You pays dear fer that when you buys shampoos and hand cream; come and do a bit of shearin' and you can have any God's amount fer nothin'. Do you know before we started shearin' my hands was as rough as a nutmeg grater? And look at me clothes, they be all clapered up with the tackle, me trousers be that stiff with all this greasy lanolin, they stands upright when I takes 'um off at night time.

'Still, about another week and we shall be done I reckon,' he said, pushing his cap back off his sweating head and giving it a good scratch. 'Ah, thas goin' well this year, we've 'ad it dry you see, and that makes a lot of difference. You get they ship all clagged up wi' rain and you got to wait till they be dryish-like uffor you can get goin'.'

'Where do the fleeces go, now that the wool staplers at Charlbury have closed down?' I asked him.

'Ah, they comes all the way from Thame to fetch these, thas the nearest place now, and I think the next one's as far away as Devon, since that un at Charlbury finished.

'I'll tel 'e what my gel, we shall be stoppin' fer tea soon. You see we works till eight o'clock, but at four we has a good half-hour break. We can have a bit of a chatter then, cos I got one or two little stories as you might like to hear. Why don't you go and ask the foreman's wife if you can have the key of the church? You'd be interested to have a look in thur I'll bet.'

'We don't get many asking for this,' she said as she handed me the great iron key.

ANOTHER KIND OF MAGIC

I walked through the overgrown church-yard, and spent a little while in the peace and quiet of the remote little church. Then made my way once more over the springy turf toward the barn.

Mark and his workmates were already digging into their dinnerbags, fetching out great hunks of home-made cake.

'My blessed,' Mark said, 'You don' half want some grub at this game, you see we leaves home affor seven in the mornin' and that'll be knockin' on fer nine affor we gets back. I don't know about these chaps' he went on, inclining his head towards his mates, 'but all I wants to do when I gets home is have a damned good wash and go off up the wooden hill to bedfordshire.'

He finished his food and came outside. 'Tis better out yer', he said, 'the smell regler gets down yu in thur.'

We climbed the steep grassy hill. I was puffing, but not Mark; he strode up the high banks like an Olympic champion.

'Wonderful view from up yer,' he said when we reached the top. 'Ah, as near to heaven as I shall ever get I recons.'

It certainly was peaceful and lovely up there on that pleasant May afternoon. The world all around was fresh and new and the greenest green. Cuckoos were calling and larks singing and the air was clear and sparkling like wine. Half-way up the hill we

had stopped to look at the source of a tiny spring, magically trickling out of the grassy bank.

'The purest clearest water in the world,' Mark said, cupping his hands to catch some. We both savoured the ice cold water. Mark splashed some over his hot face, the sun caught the falling drops, lighting them up like tiny jewels.

'I've planted a few roots of watercress, in this same spring a bit further down in the valley,' Mark said. 'I be hopin' fer a good supply of it in a year er so, you wouldn't get no frogs nor frogspawn in that, thas runnin' too fast.

'Ah, an talkin' about water reminds I of a young lad who worked on the same farm as I did at one time. He was allus called Grubby, Grubby Taylor, damned if I ever knew his right christian name. They called him that fust go off when 'e was at school. Proper dirtly little 'erbert he was too. 'Tis funny how a nickname 'ull stick. Yet when 'e growed up he was as smart and clean as any of us, but thas it, till his dyin' day, he'll allus be called Grubby Taylor by we village folks. Course thur was a big family of 'um and thur was no tap water in they days and none of yer bathrooms neither. The only way water was hotted was by the old washin' copper but I don't recon as they had their copper on a lot.

'Well, as I said, he worked on the same farm as I, and that dirty little beggar used to come to work wi' a fortnight's dirt on him. Then one day some of the older chaps thought they'd teach him a lesson, twas on a Thursday and Gaffer had gone off to market. Arter dinner they ketches Grubby and strips all his clothes off and chucks him into the old hoss trough out in the rickyard. Then they got an old brush what Carter Hicks used to brush his hosses down with and they fairly scrubbed him all over.

'The dirt was proper grammard in round his neck, you could'av planted onion seed in thur. It took four of 'um to hold him down, and 'e looked a different boy arter. That scrubbin's seemed to bring him to his senses for 'e never did seem to look quite so dirty again.

'Well, when the war broke out, off 'e goes and joins the army. And do you know my gel, he met and married a gel who's father worked in a soap factory, and arter the war Grubby joined him and the last I heard he had worked hisself up and is one of the firm's directors. I often wonders if 'e ever thinks of the day when 'e was stripped and scrubbed in the rickyard.

'Mind you,' Mark went on, 'his Gramp was a rough old fellow. I never did know how 'e earned a livin', for all 'e seemed to do was a bit of hedgin' and ditchin' and odd jobs. Yet 'e brought up a big family and he had a donkey and cart.

'But one day I see him do a very cunnin' thing.

'I was supposed to be hoein', but we'd had a sudden storm and I was shelterin' behind a hayrick. When up the road and past were I was standin' goes one of the mill wagons piled up wi' sacks of cow cake. The driver was set up front with his shoulders hunched up, he'd got a sack over his back and head cos of the pourin' rain. Well, up behind the wagon comes Grubby's Gramp, Faggot Taylor, and one of his sons. They was pushin' old Faggot's donkey cart and just as they got right up close to the mill wagon, Faggot suddenly jumps up onto the back of it. Then 'e lifted up the sheet that was coverin' the load, whips out his pocket knife and slits a great gash in one of the sacks, and into the cart falls some cow cake. Then 'e cuts open another and then another till his donkey cart was nearly full. Then 'e jumped down off the back of the mill wagon, flung the sheet back over the sacks and 'e and his son just dawdled along home with their load. 'Twas all over in less time than it have took to tell you. I wouldn't mind bettin' as that wagon driver never did find out who slit they sacks.

'Now this next story as I be goin' to tell 'e happened in our village. Mind you, twas affor we was put on the sewer; still, that was only three years ago.

'Well, one of our neighbours, Jim Potter and his missus, 'ad got Jim's Auntie Laura stayin' with 'um fer Easter. This Auntie come from London and twas the fust time as 'er had visited 'um. Course the time come when 'er had to pay a visit to their "little house" at the bottom of the garden. Well, back 'er comes a bit worried like, "Jim", 'er said, "the door of the lavatory won't shut properly, why don't you do something about it, get a key my boy and lock it up." Old Jim looked a bit puzzled like, then he said, "Auntie Laura, we've bin livin' yer fer the past twenty years and we've never 'ad a bucket of muck pinched yet, so why should I lock it up now?" '

Mark and I had a good laugh as we strolled back down the grassy bank. It was nearly time for him to start work again, and time I set out over the hills again too. When we got to where my bicycle stood, Mark said, 'Hello, you got a flat tyre my wench, that comes of leavin' yer bike in the sun. Ah, that reminds I of an old fellow who used to come round these parts sellin' sausages years ago. One day he had a puncture and he' got nothin' to mend it with and he was miles away from home, so 'e stuffed the front tube with sausages and got back that way. But you got no sausages, so we shall have to have a go at pumpin' 'im up.'

Mark blew up the tyre, which thankfully kept hard.

'Try and come over again, affor we finishes the shearin',' Mark called as I rode away.

The next few days were taken up with gathering dandelions and making them into wine. Of all the sorts I make, this seems to be the most popular. My neighbour goes to the trouble of picking out all the yellow petals to make his, but having made and savoured both sorts I think the one using the whole

flower is best, and of course not half so much trouble.

We were now into June, and the weather had turned quite cool. Only a week had passed since I had last made my way over the hills to see Mark, yet there was a great upsurge of growth everywhere. The grass fields which had not yet been cut waved and rippled like huge green seas. Gone already were the Whitsuntide Candles from the horse-chestnut trees, and a few early dog-roses trailed over the hedgerows.

'Good job you didn't put off your visit any longer,' Mark said, 'Cos we shan't be yer arter tomorrow.'

The three weeks hard work of shearing was almost

at an end. The men were working against time,
anxious to see the finish of it. Only a few sheep
waited patiently and quiet in the pen. I watched as
the last half-dozen were sheared; the last animal ran
out into the field, the men straightened their backs
and it was all over for another year.

'Ah, we shall be glad to see the backside of this
lot,' Mark said, nodding in the direction of the
great piles of fleeces stacked almost to the rafters
at one end of the barn.

'They be comin' for 'um tomorrow; we shall help
load 'um up and then we hopes to have a few days
off. Tis a bit easier on the farm once the shearin's
done. This is when the farmer "sits and takes his
ease" fer about a couple of weeks, though thur yent
much easetakin' at this lark,' he went on, 'fer gaffer
have already started cuttin' fer silage. I don't think
he's goin' in fer much hay this time.

'This yer,' Mark said turning towards the men
who had been working with him, 'is Jacko and
Thumper, old Thumper was sayin' that he'd got a
little tale to tell you but he's a bit on the shy side.
Come on Thumper, come and set down yer fer ten
minutes, we ent got nothin' to do till the foreman
comes to take we home.'

Thumper, a short stocky red faced fellow, came
over and sat down.

'Well,' he said, 'I don't rightly know where to
begin.'

'At the beginnin', you gret lappen,' Mark said grinning.

'I suppose its alright to tell you this' Thumper said nervously. 'I mean, seeing as how you might put it in that little book of yourn. But a fellow come to see we the other night and he telled it to us and we did have a laugh my missus and me.' I assured him that I had no first claim on any of my 'little stories', because someone or other had told me them. He seemed to buck up a bit when I said that and started speaking in his lovely broad dialect.

'Well, some years ago, a country bumpkin went to Burford fair. Course they didn't have many outin's in they days and this was a real treat fer him. Well, fust go off he trys his luck on the hoopla stall and after two or three goes he wins. So the man on the stall gives him a tortoise fer a prize and this yer fellow goes awf with his winnin's as proud as punch. Well, he strolls round the fair fer a bit and comes back to the hoopla again and has another go and he wins again. This time the stall-holder asked him what prize he wanted. "Ah, summut different this time", he said, "the meat in that pie I won was alright, but the crust was a bit hard, I had to throw that away".'

Just then the farm foreman came to collect the weary men. I thanked Thumper for his contribution and hoped that some day he would think of another tale to tell me.

COTSWOLD SPRING

'Next time you comes, my gel' Mark called, 'I shall be down home, tha's if you comes along within the next ten days.'

I promised to do that. We should have more time to chatter then.

My favourite recipe
for
Dandelion Wine

3 QUARTS FLOWERS
3 LB SUGAR
1 GALLON WATER
1 LB RAISINS
2 LEMONS
1 ORANGE
1 OZ YEAST

The flowers must be freshly picked. (Nip off the smallest pieces of stalk as any left on will make the wine taste bitter.) Put the flower heads into a large bowl. Bring the water to the boil and pour over the dandelions. Leave for three days, stirring once each day. Strain. Now add the sugar and the rinds only of the lemons and orange. Turn into a saucepan and boil gently for an hour. Put back into the bowl and add the juice of the lemons and orange. Leave until cool (not cold) place the yeast onto a piece of toast and place on top of the wine. Leave for three days when it should be ready to strain and put into bottles (do not quite fill bottles). Divide the raisins and slip into the bottles. Do not cork tightly until the wine has finished working. Then strain once more through paper wine filters. Made in June this is ready for drinking at Christmas.

PS. Always keep the wine covered with a cloth during the making period.

13

ALL ON A SUMMER DAY

NEARLY a year had passed since Mark and
Missus-next-door had first left their tumbledown old cottages to live in the temporary ones 'up
the top end of the village', and while Mark and his
brother had decided to stay, because of the con-
venience—Missus-next-door had settled back in her
original cottage and she had sent a message to say
that she would like me to call and see her and the
renovations.

So one sweltering August day I set off to see her.
It was hot, and very tiring with dozens of midge-
flies—thunder flies some people call them—stick-
ing to my sweating face. It was certainly very sultry
and would probably end in a thunderstorm.

With half my journey behind me I thought I'd
rest a while. A tall beech tree offered both shade
and comfort and I soon settled down with my back
against its smooth trunk. As I sat there cooling off I
remembered another weary traveller. He was an old
fellow known in these parts as 'The Witney Man',
and the expression, 'I've got the Witney Man' is
still used round here, especially by the older people
when they are feeling tired and weary, for some of

them remember the man who was given this nickname and why.

Many years ago the only method of cooking was
either by fire or paraffin oil. And one progressive
firm in Witney used to deliver paraffin oil, lamps,
stoves and wicks to many of the housewives living
in the outlying villages. One of the men who worked
for this firm was called Frank Pratley, and his de-
livery area was round Stonesfield, Coombe, Fawler
and Finstock. It was quite an event for the villagers
when once a week he came driving through the village in his horse and cart. 'Yer comes the Witney
man' they would call to one another, and they would
pick up their tin cans and jars and crowd round his
cart to be served.

He was a kind man and if any of them had trouble
in fixing a lamp wick, or their stove smoked, he
would always put it right for them.

Well, after one hot trying day Frank Pratley
turned towards home. He got as far as Norlie
(Northleigh) common, which looked cool and in-
viting. He tethered his horse to a tree so that he
could get a good feed of grass, then stretched himself out in the sweet-smelling bracken and went off
to sleep. Back in Witney the owner of the paraffin
shop had begun to get a bit worried. It was 7.30
p.m. and Pratley not back from his journey. So he
asked two of the other men to take a horse and cart
and go and look for him. Anything could have hap-

pened to man, horse and cart, for it wasn't like Pratley to be late.

Well, they found him curled up on Norlie common sleeping as peaceful as a baby. Of course he never lived it down, they were always teasing him about it. And after that episode, anyone who felt tired and listless had the complaint known as 'The Witney Man'. And I had definitely got that complaint on this scorching hot day.

I wasn't going to curl up and go to sleep, but it was peaceful sitting there under the big tree, along the quiet road which would eventually lead to the hamlet where Missus-next-door lived. In the field opposite to where I was resting, men were busy harvesting. A giant scarlet combine charged up and down the field at a fair pace, stopping every now and then to discharge its load of golden grain into a waiting trailer. It all seemed so easy, this way of harvesting—at least much easier than in the old days.

I thought as I sat there what knowledgeable men farmers and farm workers have to be. They have to understand drainage, medicine, mechanics as well as soil and seeds, beasts and weather. It certainly was a lovely day. Such beauty there was all around, with every field and fold throwing up a different hue. It was like gazing at a giant patchwork, of lovely muted greens and golds and rich brown earth, and the stone walls which part the fields running like a lace thread across the wold.

There were wild flowers on the verge-sides—gay mauve scabious, candy-striped mallow, purple vetch and yellow bedstraw. It was one of those days when every sound is 'sharp set' as we call it. I could hear a dog barking way off in some lonely farmyard, and rooks cawing, but I couldn't see them. A church clock down in the valley chimed the hour of three, it was time I set off over the hills again.

A lovely smell of freshly baked cakes met me as I walked into Missus-next-door's spick and span cottage. I sniffed. 'Yes', she said, 'I've made yer favourite, seedy en't it? I remembered you said you liked seedy, and I've made a bit of what I calls me special gingerbread too.'

I was glad of the hot sweet tea, and her cakes were delicious. 'Ah, I'll give 'e the receipt affor you goes if you'd like it,' she said, after I'd complimented her.

The improvements made to Missus-next-door's cottage were marvellous, and she was very pleased to show me round. 'Mind you', she rambled on, 'that electric stove took a bit of getting used to, arter cooking with nothing but paraffin and that old fire-oven fer years; but I manages.'

'I can't really understand why old Mark and his brother don't want to come back', she prattled on, 'what could you want better than this? Course I suppose when you comes to think of it, it ent so convenient as the one they be in, what with 'e havin' to dry his jackuts and things.'

'They're getting on well with the harvest round here', I said to her, after we'd settled down to another cup of tea.

'Ah', she said, 'I was a-watchin' 'um out in that thur field only yes'day and I thought how different it was to what 'twas a few years ago, before the combines, when a good farmer had got six or seven great ricks in his rickyard. Course they don't have nothin' like that now-a-days, I used to enjoy a bit of threshin' work, we reckoned on that round yer to buy a bit of warm clothes fer winter. When that old threshing machine drawed into farmer Baines' yard we women knowed as we was all right fer two or three weeks work, cos every farmer in the village would have his threshin' done once the threshin' tackle and the men got yer. We used to start work just after seven in the mornin' and keep on till half past four in the arternoon, with an hour break at midday. My word, that fust days threshin' nearly killed we, tossin' they sheaves all day. 'Twasn't so bad when you was right on top of the rick, pitchin' 'um down, but when you got three parts down the rick and you had to toss they sheaves up on to the threshin' drum, that was when it made yer muscles ache. I didn't mind when we was doing wheat ricks, but when we got on to barley that was awful, full of dust, and they barley hales* used to stick to yer clothes, nearly sent you mad a-scratchin'. When

* Barley hales are the little whiskers on the end of the seed

176

you got home the best thing to do was to strip awf and pick 'um out yer vest and knickers. Mind you', she went on, 'we used to have a damned good laugh —ah, and talking about strippin', I remembers the time when George Franklin took all his clothes awf when we was threshin' up at High Barn Farm once, bitter cold day it was too.

'Course when they ricks had been stood in that rickyard fer months, they used to get that full of rats and when we got towards the bottom you had to watch out. The farmer and any kids what was about used to stand thur waitin' with great sticks and try and kill 'um as they rushed out; the dogs used to catch 'um too.

'Well, on this day as I be tellin' you about, we'd got right down to the last few sheaves and nobody thought thur was any more rats left. Suddenly old George tosses up a sheaf and then 'e lets out such a yell, "E's gone up me trousers", 'e shouts, and 'e starts dancin' about in the yard tryin' to shake the animal down, but we could see that the rat was up near his backside. Thur was such a yellin' and a-shoutin', then the farmer hollers "take 'um awf, take 'um awf or 'e'll eat you alive", and old George was fair goin' mad screamin' and dancin' about.

' "That's it", Bert Abbot shouts, "take 'um awf affor 'e eats yer doings." That done it, 'e does no more than strips awf, naked as the day 'e was born, and awf runs the rat across the yard with the dogs followin' after it. Ah, old George was lucky not to be bit, but I should think with all the noise we was makin' the poor animal was frit to death.

'After that we took particular notice to tie the bottoms of our trousers with a piece of bagtie string. Well they was our husbands' trousers really, thur was not such things as women's trousers in they days. Well if thur was, we couldn't afford 'um just fer a few weeks threshin'.'

Missus-next-door refilled our cups. And the beautiful summer afternoon wore on; it was as cool as a church in the stone cottage.

'I'll tell 'e another little tale' she said, 'thas if you got time to listen.'

I assured her I'd got all the time in the world. I've learned over the years that if country folk want to talk the best thing to do is to let them, for you're sure to hear something worth while.

'You might think that this is a bit far fetched', she went on, 'but its gospel truth; happened to my eldest brother it did when 'e was about seventeen. You see 'e worked for a pig killing man and sometimes his gaffer would give 'im a bit of meat or offal to bring home to our mother. We was a big family and her was very glad of it. Well, one night just as 'e was leaving work his boss ses to 'im, "yer be Ted take these chitlins home." He'd got no bag or basket to put 'um in so 'e slips 'um into his trouser pocket, not realisin' thur was a hole in it. Now on

his way home 'e catches up with a young girl from
our village, walkin' home from work her was, and
our Ted being a bit sweet on her gets awf his bike
and walks alongside her, trying to get off with her
like. They hadn't bin walkin' very long when the

179

girl suddenly shrieks out "what's that", pointin' to a piece of chitlin that was danglin' below our Ted's trouser leg. Quick as a flash he whips out his pen-knife, cuts awf the piece that was showin' and chucks it over the hedge, and the poor girl fell down in a dead faint, and, do you know, 'er never spoke to our Ted again after that.'

Missus-next-door and I roared with laughter over her tales. 'Have you got time just fer a short un?' she asked, 'then I shall have to start cookin' fer my old man, 'e gets in just after five and 'e likes his meal on the table when 'e comes in.

'Well now, this happened at one of our Women's Institute meetings a few years back. I shan't tell you the woman's name although her bin dead this ten year; but on the night I felt that embarrassed for the poor woman, though I don't think 'er ever knew what 'er said. But I thinks some of 'um in the audience did, the way they laughed.

'Twas like this you see, this yer woman was the one chosen as the deligate to go to the Annual general meeting what they holds in London every year, and the person that goes has to give a report about it to her own W.I. So 'er starts talkin' about the trip and the meetin' and her said "We was all settled in the Albert Hall and then the meetin' started with the hymn Jerusalem and we all sang out with lust". Well, I ask you my dear, we don't do that sort of thing at W.I. meetings now, do we?'

'Not at ours anyhow' I assured her.

'Now about this yer cake receipt you wanted, I'll just write it out for you', and she scribbled away quietly for a few minutes.

We'd had a wonderful afternoon and I promised that I would come and see her again one day. But that day never came. Three weeks later dear Missus-next-door was walking home in the dimpsey light, well on the side of the road too, when a car driven recklessly by a young fellow knocked her down and she died three days later without regaining consciousness.

I often think of her, and the wonderful stories she told me. She loved what she called 'a bit of company', a bit of company that we often shared. And I still have the two nice blue 'vawses' that she gave me. I thought it would be a fitting tribute to her to finish this chapter with her 'receipt' for what she called 'me special gingerbread'.

Missus-Next-Door's
Special Gingerbread

Sift together 8 oz of S.R. flour, half a tablespoon of ground ginger and half a teaspoon of mixed spice. Into a heavy pan put 4 oz margarine, 4 oz soft brown sugar, 4 oz golden syrup and 4 oz of black treacle. Heat gently until sugar dissolves. Cool a little. Beat together one egg and a gill of milk. Add this and the melted ingredients to the flour and mix well. Pour into a well-lined meat tin and bake in the middle of the oven for 1¼ hours until firm to touch. Gas No. 3 or electricity 333. Allow to cool before removing from tin.

14

WORLD WITHOUT END

FOR a number of years my old friend Mark had threatened to give up his job. He'd stayed on long past retiring age, because his boss kept saying that he couldn't find anyone to replace him. The truth was that if Mark did retire, his boss knew that he would have to employ two men to do the 'shuppering'.

But a couple of bad winters, coupled with the fact that he had developed acute arthritis in his right hand, which Mark attributed to years of whacking in posts with his heavy folding bar, helped him to make up his mind. So I was not surprised when he told me 'I've jacked it all up and so have gaffer.'

'What! Your boss given up farming,' I cried.

'No, just the ship,' he said, 'he couldn't get a shuppard nowhere. Tis a seven day a week job you see, my wench, you got to go and have a look at 'um even on a Sunday, and the young uns wun't have it not at any price. So 'e sent 'um all off to Bicester market and finished with 'um altogether.

'Course,' Mark went on, 'I shall have to do a bit of summut, if its only to get some beer and baccy money. Any road, I couldn't abide not doin' nothin'. But I byent rushin' into anything. Thurs bin two or

three arter I already, to go gyardnin' for 'um, but I
byent goin' to have much of that this wet weather. I
shall be like they old hedgehogs, I shall hibernate
and come out fresh and eager in the spring.'

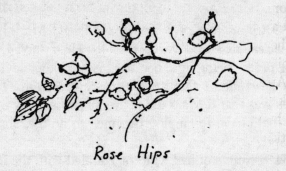

Rose Hips

We were now well into November and the
weather had turned cold and wet. Almost silently
the yellowing leaves were falling from the great
elms, fluttering lifelessly to the ground to lay de-
jectedly at our feet. It was the end of their life,
those patchy yellow leaves that had gladdened our
hearts in the spring with their delicate greenery.
Some people get sad over Autumn, but I like to
think that its really just the beginning of another
year's growth. There were still golden leaves cling-
ing to the beech branches; soon they too would fall,
only to be scooped up again by eager gardeners.
The only other colours in the hedgerows were a few
scarlet hips and a glint of gold here and there where
gorse bushes had established themselves.

'You knaws what they ses about gorse don't you', Mark said, after I had remarked on the lovely blooms for the time of year.

'Kissing's out of fashion when the gorse is not in bloom. But tis always in bloom, at least you can allus find a flower 'er two bloomin', no matter what time of the year it is; and you knaws kissin's never out of fashion,' he said good-humouredly.

'And talkin' about colour, the other day when I took the dogs for a walk, I see summut growin' in the hedge as I never noticed affor, well not in this particular part of the country any road. Course I recognised what twas, though its years since I saw any.' We were strolling down the lane behind the shepherd's cottage, the dogs running excitedly in front.

'Yer tis then,' Mark cried, 'Spindleberry en't it? Now thas what I calls a nice bright colour.' The gaudy, pinky yellow berries hung like little lanterns on the almost leaf-bare branches. We picked a few sprays.

'Very hard wood the spindle tree is', Mark went on, 'thas what it was used for years ago, to make spindles, the sort they used for weaving. Mind you, you don't want to encourage it to grow near yer garden; attracts the black fly summut dreadful, that do.

'This is what I bin fillin' me time with fer the past few wiks,' Mark said as he proudly showed me a section of dry stone walling. He had almost re-built the entire wall that circled his garden. It looked as good as if it had been done by an experienced tradesman.

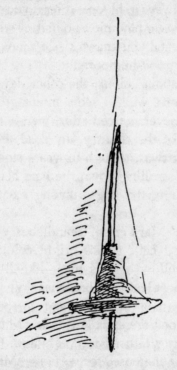

'Where did you learn how to do that?' I exclaimed, amazed at the workmanship.

'Ah, I watched the old fellows,' he replied. 'You see, thurs a tidy bit of dry stwon wallin' round these parts, specially on the farm wur I worked. And some mornin's when we got to work arter we'd had a heavy rain overnight, like as not thur'd be a piece of wall fell down. And as soon as our gaffer got to hear about it 'ed shout, "send for Break-spear". He was a retired stone mason what lived over at Delly Green, and he was glad to do a bit of work now and then. Wonderful craftsman he was, twas a pleasure to watch him at work; he'd got an eye as keen as an eagle when it come to cuttin' and shapin' stwons.

'You see, you got to get um to fit in right, and he could pick up a stwon from a gret pile and place it just right, sometimes without havin' to chip even an inch awf.

'I often used to watch him at work. We was very good pals too, 'e used to set along wi' I to have his victuals. And sometimes 'ed get on about his younger days. Mind you, 'e bin dead and gone this twenty years—lived till 'e was ninety-odd though. He started work when 'e was twelve year old and fer years 'e walked backurds and forrods from Bladon to Oxford—six days a wik fer 1½d. a day— apprentice 'e was, and ended up as one of the finest stone masons anywur round yer. I expect, in his time, he'd worked on every college in Oxford. I don't mean buildin' 'um, I means repairin' the stwon-work, although now I comes to think of it he did help to build one of they newish uns. And I'll bet thur's many a wall or buildin' whats standin' today as he helped to build, good solid cotswold stwon places, and they'll still be standin' long arter you and I be gone.'

'How do you begin to build a dry stone wall?' I asked.

'First,' he said, 'you must start right at the bottom. Even a wall has to have footin's, not as deep as a house mind you, about three or four inches below ground. Then you lays some good big flat stwons fer the base, like this.' He paused, showing me a piece that he had just started to build.

'You see, when you starts, its like two walls, but as you works up you binds 'um together here and there with a very big stwon, what they calls "threws", and that sort of ties it together. Then you fills the middle up wi' all yer small stwons and rubble. And you'll notice, as the wall gets higher it gets very slightly narrower. Then you gets what we calls an "edger", thas a nice shaped un, they be kept for finishin' awf, by a gateway or end of a wall.

'This is what I shapes the stwons with', he said, picking up a rather clumsy looking hammer; the head was sort of boat-shaped. 'Old Jim Breakspear give I that', Mark said, 'twas one 'ed used fer years. Then you tops the wall up with these copin' stwons or double coulters, as we calls 'um. See, you places 'um upright like this,' Mark said demonstrating how he finished off the wall top.

'Mind you, handlin' stwons all day don't half

188

make yer fingers sore, cos you can't wear gloves 'er nothin'. But', Mark went on, 'I think wallin's a very satisfying job, you be sort of creatin' summut; well thas how I feels when I be doin' this. When you comes to think of it, my wench, I was all they years shupperin' and I really ent got nothin' to show for it, only me shupherd's crook and a gammy hand. But a man what builds a house or a wall or a church have left his mark, summut as you can remember him by,' he said seriously.

'How do you manage to work with your bad hand?' I enquired.

'Ah, some days it plays I up that much as I can't even hold a pen, leave alone a stwon. Then other days, when tis dry-like, I gets on quite well. Mind you I takes me time, thur yent no cause fer I to do it if I don't feel like it,' he told me laughingly.

'I had to smile to meself 'tother mornin'' he went on, changing the subject, 'thurs two old fellows, Ted Oliver and Bert Norridge what lives up the road a bit, and most days one or 'tother comes down yer and watches I, and gives a bit of advice too. Well 'issday they met just about wur we be standin' now, and Ted Oliver ses "Wur be you awf to this morning' then Bert?" and old Bert said, "I byent goin' nowur I be just come back." I had to chuckle to meself, that did sound so funny to I.'

Mark picked up a piece of fossil-filled stone and turned it over in his great hand. 'I'll bet that stwon's thousands and thousand of years old, look at all they tiny shells fossilled in thur. Ah, stwons a wonderful thing when you come to think of it, and course this county's famous for its quarries, though thur yent so many being worked as thur was. Do you know, my wench, the stwon what they used to build St. Paul's mostly come from this area. I suppose any cotswold building fer miles around was built from local quarried stwons. And you must admit they buildings be lastin' memorials to the craftsmen who built 'um—summut that generations of people have looked at. And folks 'ull still be lookin' at 'um fer a good many years to come.'

Before I left Mark was already chipping away at the stones, fitting them into the wall. I watched him, his head slightly on one side as he surveyed his handiwork. Here was a truly contented man. His needs were few, yet he was rich in character and wisdom. And having seen the beautiful dry stone wall that he was re-creating, with all the skill and knowledge that he had gleaned over the years, I felt sure that if people didn't remember him as a shepherd they would remember him for the way he built this wall.

15

WHITEY SMITH

I FIRST met Whitey Smith in a pub; I was de-livering the wartime ration of cigarettes and crisps, from the wholesale grocers where I worked, to the Inn where Whitey could often be found prop-ping up the bar. He was getting on for seventy then, and had worked hard for well over fifty years, so he reckoned that he'd earned his half pint and daily chatter with the other old worthies who made the bar parlour their meeting place.

The Inn Keeper said to me one day, 'That's the fellow to tell a tale, I can never remember 'um, but 'e reels 'um off by the dozen, buy him half a pint and he'll go on fer hours.'

The trouble was, in those wartime days I was usually pushed for time—six long weary years they were, and I was very glad when the time came to hand the lorry back to its former driver, a soldier re-turning from the wars, and I was able to settle down to being a housewife once more. Then one day I suddenly thought of Whitey and his tales, and hied me off to see if the old fellow was still propping up the bar in 'The Black Boy'.

There he was, still in the same place. His hair was thinner than when I'd last seen him, otherwise he'd

changed very little. I was given a great welcome.

'Ju remember 'er,' Whitey said to the other customers, 'used to come round durin' the war, drivin' that gret lorry—I've sin 'er carry a two hundern-weight bag of sugar on 'er back into that old bake-house next door—she carried it as if twas a couple of pounds,' and they oh'd and ah'd and remembered.

I told him that I'd come to hear some of the stories that I'd never had time to listen to before, and Whitey, the great talker that he was, settled for 'something tu wet me whistle' and started—

'I'll tell you 'ow I come by me nickname fust go awf—I was christened Herbert you see, arter me uncle, but I bin called Whitey fer years, on account of the colour of this old thatch of mine. Ah, it bin snow white like this since I was seventeen, went white overnight it did, as true as I set yer that is.

'You see, I was a learnin' to be a carter, and Sid Baker, 'e was over I on this biggish farm wur we was employed. Well, when we come home from the fields at night, old Sid 'ud clear off home and leave I to feed and water the hosses. Well on this particular day, well twas night-time really, we comes home from ploughin' and as usual off goes old Sid.

'I goes out to the well to draw up some water for the hosses and before you could say Jack Robinson I'd slipped on the wet ground and went headfust down the well. I hit the bottom then struck out as

if I was swimmin' in the river and comes to the
surface—course twas as black as pitch down thur. I
hollered and shouted but nobody heard. I thought
I'd had it, for twas a deep well and the stone sides
was damp and slippery without much of a place to
hang on to. I kept tryin' to climb the wall of the
well, keepin' me eyes on a little bit of half light at
the top. But as fast as I climbed I slipped back into
the water again, till I was damn near exhausted.
Well, I couldn't tell you what happened arter that,
but when I "come to" I was lying on the muck
heap in the yard; and thas wur Gaffer found I when
'e and his wife drove in from market.

'They took I home—I had a couple of days in bed
—and when I got up me hair was as white as it is
now and thas fifty odd years ago.'

Whitey paused for a swig and went on, 'I was
a-tellin' this same tale to one a they clever sort of
town fellas one day, and 'e ses to I a bit cocky-like,
"How long were you down the well young man?"
And I answers him pretty smartish and said "I
dun't know sir, I never looked at me watch", ha ha,
'e never asked I any more silly questions arter that.'

Somebody called for drinks all round and the
'customers' settled down again as Whitey rambled
on. 'And I'll tell 'e another funny thing that happened to I. I was puttin' some barbed wire fencin'
round one of Gaffer's fields; you see we'd had a lot
of trouble with the cattle gettin' out. I was getting

on very well with the fencing when suddenly I drops me hammer and as I bent down to pick it up I caught me trousers on the barbed wire and damn near tore the backside out.

'Well, I couldn't go all the way home like that, twasn't decent, so I goes up to the farmhouse and asked Gaffer's wife if 'er could cobble it up, rough like, just to last I till I got home at night.

' "Come on in Whitey" 'er said, "and bend over that chair and I'll see what I can do." Mind you, 'er was a bit heavy handed with that thur needle, two or three times 'er jabbed I in the backside.

'Well, when 'er'd finished I stands up and ses to 'er, "thank you kindly Mam, I be most grateful, and I'll do the same fer you if you be ever likewise fixed."

'Her looks I strait in the eye and said "I sincerely hope that occasion never arises Whitey."

'Mind you, I didn't mean what I said, about doin' the same fer 'er, but I could hardly stop from bustin' out laughin'.

'Then thur was the time when my young nephew come down this way to work, durin' the war it was, when the government used to send the workers wur they was needed most. Well, young George, that was his name, was about eighteen at the time, and his Mother, my missus's sister, thought it 'ud be a good thing if 'e come and lodged with us. Twas the lad's first visit to the country—lived in London all

his life 'e had. It was one a they real hot days when young George arrived, a Sunday if I remembers rightly. Well 'e goes indoors to say hello to my missus, then comes out into the garden to I and ses "Uncle", 'e ses, "Where's your toilet?" so I ses to 'im "wurs the what?" "Well where's your lavatory then?" he said, a bit urgent like. So I ses to 'im, "ah, that's the place, that little old stwon place thur at the bottom of the gyarden—just behind that thur boxbush."

'So down the gyarden path 'e goes a bit quick like, but 'e comes back again strait away and said "I can't go in there uncle tis full of flies", so I looks at me watch and ses to 'im, "Ah-h thee try and hang on fer ten minutes, missus is goin' to dish up the dinner, they'll all come up yer then", and I laughed. Course 'e didn't know how to take what I'd said and I thinks

it put 'im off 'is dinner, for 'e never 'et a thing, but 'e soon got used to they flies—you has to when you lives in the country. We used to hang Elderflower branches up in the dyke (lavatory) years ago, they was supposed to keep the flies away. Nowadays my missus takes one a they airysole things down with 'er. Fust time 'er done that, 'er squirted it so much as 'er sat thur, 'er nearly passed out 'erself. Come staggerin' up the path as if 'er was drunk 'er did. Damn that, I'd rather put up wi' the flies meself.

'Well now,' Whitey went on, looking at his pocket watch, 'we ent got a lot more time today, otherwise the landlord will be chucking us out, it looks as if we just got time fer a short 'un.'

'Ah-h and a quick 'un,' one of his mates said, and I nodded to the landlord to fill the glasses again.

'What about the caretaker story?' he said as he brought the drinks to us.

'Oh ah, I'd fergot that 'un,' Whitey said, smacking his lips over the fresh cool beer.

'Now this happened over at Tanfield Bottom a few years back; I knows its gospel 'cos it was my second cousin and his missus as was the caretakers thur at the time, and all they 'ad to do was keep this big country house tidy like and show folks round—they as might want to buy it.

'Mind you, they was new at this caretakin' lark and thur first "customer" was a portly gentleman who seemed quite interested in the property. After he'd had a good look round he turned to Fred, me second cousin, and said, "How many windows face north and where's the W.C. ?"

'Course old Fred didn't know what 'e meant so 'e looks at his wife and 'er whispered to him "Wesleyan

chapel you fool". So then Fred turned to the gentleman and said, very important like, "Thur are five
windows that face north Sir, and the nearest W.C.
is half a mile away. I went thur six months ago, but
I had to stand up all night so I ent bothered since."
Oh dear,' Whitey went on, 'we've had many a
chuckle over that I can tell you. Now I'd best get
off home, my missus got a bacon and onion puddin'
on fer our dinner, 'er wunt like it if I be late.' He
called cheerio to his mates. Then he turned to me.

'Why dun't you come down home along wi' I' he
said, 'I expect I could think of a few more stories,
arter I've had me dinner like.'

'Tell you what Whitey,' I said to him, 'I'll have a
look round the village and find somewhere in the
cool to eat my sandwiches, then I'll come along to
your house and meet your wife, in about an hour's
time.'

'Ah, perhaps thas the best idea,' he replied as he
turned for home. 'And don't ferget tis the last
cottage on the left-hand side down Spittalls Lane.'

The village itself was small and scattered, yet the
church was a huge magnificent building, built on the
brow of a hill rising up from the river Evenlode.
Two elderly men sat on a bench under the giant Elm
trees, dark and heavy with summer leaf, and down
the lane the blackberry flowers and white convolvulus
climbed and looped their way over the hedge-rows.

Whitey was on the look out for me. His cottage

was very picturesque, built of Cotswold stone and roofed with lichen-covered Stonesfield slates.

'My Grandfather most likely quarried they very slats (slates) his-self, out of one of the local mines,' Whitey told me proudly as we stood and surveyed his little castle. 'You see, he worked in the next village, ah, quite a lot of the men hereabouts was employed in they old slat mines. Course twas a hard job and the conditions was a bit grim too. You see the mines, or pits as some folks call 'em, was only about three or four foot high and the men often had to work all day long a-creepin' along on thur hands and knees, peckin' out all the waste soil and small stwons to get to the rocks. Then they loaded these rocks, gret stwons they was, on to a thing called a "jack barrow", they then was hauled to the surface. And then the rocks was laid out all over the ground and the village folk used to pray for good, hard, frosty winters. You see that was what split the rocks into slats, and sometimes the men would pour water over the rocks to make sure the frost got right through and split 'um properly. Mind you,' he went on, 'the slats had to be shaped properly afterwards and that was a very skilled job too. The men what done this often set up a little bit of shelter in the field, like a little workshop it was. Sometimes twas just a couple of hurdles covered with straw, anything to keep out the cold wind. Then they'd get a gret big stwon that served as a work bench and the slat was rested on this while the man tapped away turnin' out a slat shaped summut like a luggage label only a lot bigger, then he'd make a small hole in the top, then when the tiler come to fix the slat on a roof he would drive a small wooden peg into that hole so that the slat could be hung on a lath when it was in its right position on the roof.

'Ah,' Whitey went on, 'they slats had names accordin' to thur size, I knowed 'um all at one time, thur was "Cussems" and "Long Becks", "Muffities" and "Long Elevens", but I can't remember no more. I en't quite sure when the last Stwonsfold (Stonesfield) slats was quarried—pity they dun't do it now, but perhaps they run out of the right sort of rock in this district. Course the only way you can get hold of any now is when an old barn or cottage is pulled down. Worth thur weight in gold damn-near they be.

'Course thur must have bin thousands of tons of 'um quarried round yer at one time. Now the only thing left is all they hummocks and mounds in the fields; thur's four or five big 'uns just as you goes out of Stwonsfold. They piles be all the waste stuff what was left behind after the men had dug the rocks out. I went into one a they mines some years ago,' he said, 'just to have a look like. Damp and dark it was, and creepy—I was glad to get out in the fresh air agen I'll tell 'e.

'Well my gel, I thinks I'll go and have forty

winks now; I do most afternoons, so do my old lady. You come and see I agen one of these dinner-times, you knows wur to find I, in "The Black Boy". We never did get round to any more story tellin' this afternoon did us? Still, thur's always another day, ent thur?' he said, as he waved me goodbye.

But it was mid-winter before I saw Whitey again. I'd had a card from his wife to say that he was 'in bed with his leg', but that he wanted to see me.

I found him propped up in a huge brass bed. He looked frail and tired, and his white hair stuck out rough and untidy like an old bird's nest.

'Ah my gel,' he said after I had asked after his health, 'I don't think I shall be able to get down to "The Black Boy" again. You must remember I be goin' on fer ninety five, I be well past me four score years and ten. I've bin lucky really, this is the fust time in me life as I've bin bed-bound'. He went on, his pale eyes watering, 'I wanted to tell you that thur's going to be a village do at Stwonsfold later on this year, and when old Ted Gammage come to see I the other day he said that the farmer who owns the only slat mine what 'ent bin filled in is goin' to let folks go down it, fer a small fee. Not for his-self mind you, but fer church funds. And I thought as you'd like the chance to see down one, bein' as you be interested in that sort of thing. Mind you, the numbers 'ull have to be limited, so you'll have to get yer oar in quick, cos they reckons that this might be the last time that the public 'ull be allowed to go down.' Here Whitey paused for breath. He went on, 'all the other pits have bin filled in and blocked up to make 'um safe-like, but somehow this un was left. Mind you I thinks it was a very wise thing, otherwise the present generation 'ud never knowed what the working conditions was like.'

I thanked Whitey for the news, then turned to his wife to remark on the wonderful patchwork quilt that covered the bed. It was a beautiful thing and an absolute galaxy of colour. She told me proudly that her grandmother had started it, then her own mother had had a go, and she herself had finished it off.

'This here's a bit of my granny's wedding dress,' she said, pointing to a blue-grey patch of shot silk,' 'and this was a piece of my mother's wedding dress', she went on, moving her hand across to a bit of sprigged muslin. 'Course that had to have a piece of firmer material on the back of that. And this here's a scrap from my wedding frock and further over here's a bit from our daughter's; lovely brocade it was, looked like a queen in it she did. Ah, there's memories of four generations sewed into this old quilt, though who 'ull want it when we be gone I don't know,' she said sadly.

The Church festival that Whitey had told me about, which was to include the reopening of the old slate mine, was held the following May. By then Whitey had moved to 'pastures new', having died quietly in his sleep about three weeks after I'd visited him.

The trip down the old slate mine was certainly worth while. We descended the thirty foot shaft by means of two long ladders which were roped together, and to me it seemed that we were going to the very bowels of the earth. The bottom of the shaft was damp with spring water, gently oozing from the sides of the shaft, which was skilfully built with local stone; and from where we stood, waiting for our guide, it looked as if we were standing at the bottom of a great well.

We worked our way along the narrow tunnel, which was never more than four feet high and in some places only three feet, and only about five feet wide. Some crawled crabwise while others went along on hands and knees; soon we were covered in thick yellow mud. Most of us carried torches, but the men who once toiled down there must have had to work with the aid of lanterns.

Our guide explained the working conditions, which must have been appalling, to say nothing of the pay which was 8/–d. a week at the time when most of the pits closed around 1910. Apparently most of the rock was hewn out of the pits from about October to January, and men used to walk for miles to Stonesfield during that period to try and get a few week's work there. The rocks were laid out on the surface, and if the weather was mild and dry they would be carefully covered with any vegetation that was available, so that the pit moisture wouldn't dry out; if this happened, the slate flaked off in layers and was useless as a roof tile. As soon as the frosty weather came the vegetation was taken off, and if a very severe frost was imminent the men of the village would be called out during the night (by the ringing of the church bells) to pour water over the rocks.

But the men who worked down the pits envied the fellows who cut and shaped the tiles, for their work lasted all the year round. Sitting in their little huts made from hurdles and straw they turned out slates at £2.0.0. a 1,000. At the turn of the century there were two such men employed here at this job —both elderly and loth to show anyone else their trade, for a younger man working faster could have put them out of work.

Around 1910 it was decided that it was uneconomical to work the pits and one by one they closed down. But the strong men of Stonesfield (and they must have been strong men to put up with those conditions) left their mark all over the country: on castles, colleges, cottages and cowsheds, in the form of lovely, grey, lichen-covered Stonesfield slates.

CONCLUSION

A FEW weeks after the completion of this book, I was asked to join the cast of the B.B.C.'s famous long-running serial 'The Archers'. My part is that of an ordinary cheerful village woman. Such a person can be found in any English village, as indeed can the rest of the Archer cast. And as *Another Kind of Magic* deals with the lives of country folk, I didn't want the book to go to press without paying tribute to the painstaking accuracy and attention to detail that goes into the making of 'The Archers'. In fact, the script writers and producer are so exact in their interpretation of country life today that the whole story could easily be happening in any village in this green and pleasant land of ours.

The farming people and their kin, the village shop with its harmless chatter, the pub—a popular meeting place for the menfolk—the threat of closing the village school 'meals on wheels', the old people's club, good crops, bad crops, the knowledge and experience of the older workers blending with the modern methods of the younger generation, all these help to make the serial a true picture of the present day.

CONCLUSION

Until I joined this happy group of actors I had no idea of the amount of hard work that goes into making such a programme successful. One thing to which, rightly, great importance is attached is getting the right sound effects. These are taken from a huge library of tape recordings made from actual country sounds—Sunday morning church bells, rooks in the elms, lambs bleating, the cry of a dog fox, the harsh sound of a tractor or a harvester, all combining to make the programme as true to life as possible.

Having always lived in the country, and worked on a farm for several years, I feel quite at home with 'The Archers'. In *Another Kind of Magic* you will have met ordinary, earthy countrymen and women, as I met them on the farms and in the villages of Oxfordshire and Gloucestershire. And in 'The Archers' programme you can meet their like again, very faithfully portrayed.

OXFORD

MORE OXFORD PAPERBACKS

Details of a selection of other books follow. A complete list of
Oxford Paperbacks, including The World's Classics,
Twentieth-Century Classics, OPUS, Past Masters, Oxford
Authors, Oxford Shakespeare, and Oxford Paperback
Reference, is available in the UK from the General Publicity
Department, Oxford University Press, Walton Street, Oxford,
OX2 6DP.

In the USA, complete lists are available from the Paperbacks
Marketing Manager, Oxford Paperbacks, 200 Madison
Avenue, New York, NY 10016.

THE BRENSHAM TRILOGY

John Moore

New introduction by Asa Briggs

The three much-loved books in The Bresham Trilogy—
Portrait of Elmbury, Brensham Village, and *The Blue Field*—
are now available for the first time in one volume. Written
between 1945 and 1948, they are all set in or nearby the old
town of Tewkesbury in Gloucestershire where the author, John
Moore, lived, and many of his entertaining characters are
based on real people. Asa Briggs provides a new introduction.
For lovers of rural nostalgia and social history, this authentic
portrait of English rural life is a must.

'One of the best writers on the English countryside'
Harold Nicholson

OUR VILLAGE

Mary Russell Mitford

Illustrated by Joan Hassall

Introduction by Margaret Lane

'Of all the situations for a constant residence, that which appears to me most delightful is a little village, far in the country . . . with inhabitants whose faces are as familiar to us as flowers in our garden.' Mary Russell Mitford lived in just such a village, Three Mile Cross in Berkshire, for more than thirty years. She drew on her observations of the locality for many short essays, the best of which appear in this book, which give a unique picture of country life in the early years of the nineteenth century.

THE DILLEN

Memories of a Man of Stratford-upon-Avon

Edited by Angela Hewins

Foreword by Ronald Blythe

George Hewins was born in a Stratford doss-house at the zenith of the Victorian age. He grew up in desperate poverty, barely literate, underfed and under-sized (hence his nickname of 'the dillen' or runt). But George did possess one extraordinary gift: he was a storyteller of genius in the old oral tradition. *The Dillen* is his story, told to his grandson's wife as he approached his hundredth year.

'It is funny and heartbreaking by turn, packed with incidents and curiosities.' *Sunday Times*

'It takes the reader by the scruff of the neck and forces him to taste the food, smell the smells, agree to the tricks and breathe the air of a cheerful, dreadful England which would do for you if it could.' Ronald Blythe

STILL GLIDES THE STREAM

Flora Thompson

Like her well-loved trilogy *Lark Rise to Candleford*, this book depicts the vanished life of the countryside which Flora Thompson knew as a child in the 1880s. Cast in a fictional form, it is an enchanting portrait of an Oxfordshire village and its inhabitants around the time of Queen Victoria's Golden Jubilee.

'reading it is a perfect pleasure' Benny Green

A COUNTRY CALENDAR
AND OTHER WRITINGS

Flora Thompson

Selected and edited by Margaret Lane

Illustrated by Clare Roberts

Admirers of Flora Thompson will welcome this volume of her writings selected and edited from her uncollected or unpublished papers. It includes Margaret Lane's biographical essay; *Heatherley*, a lightly disguised account of Flora Thompson's life in Grayshott, Hampshire before she married; a selection of her observations and other writings; some of her poems; and photographs and line drawings.

'A must for Flora Thompson addicts and a superb introduction to the uninitiated.' *The Times*

FARMER'S GLORY

A. G. Street

Woodcuts by Gwen Raverat

Preface by Pamela Street

This portrait of farming life recalls the agricultural practices and traditions of the first quarter of this century. First published in 1932, *Farmer's Glory* was an immediate popular success and has since become a classic account of country life.

'An enthralling picture of rural life . . . It will go on the shelf of my library with Cobbett's *Rural Rides*, White's *Natural History of Selborne* . . . on my favourite shelf, in fact.'
Compton Mackenzie

'His book is the best on English farm-life . . . that it has ever been my pleasure to read.' H. E. Bates

THE ENGLISH YEAR

Chosen by Geoffrey Grigson

Illustrated by John Constable

Geoffrey Grigson has composed a portrait of the English year
from the writings of poets, painters, parsons, and many others
who have recorded their impressions, in letters and journals, of
our matchless countryside and climate.

Contributors include: John Clare, Dorothy Wordsworth,
Gilbert White, Francis Kilvert, Thomas Gray, Thomas Hardy,
Gerard Manley Hopkins, Samuel Taylor Coleridge, and James
Woodforde.

'an elegant compilation of short notes on nature and the
weather from English diaries and letters, chiefly of the last two
centuries, that offers many pleasures.' *Guardian*